ISLAM AT THE CROSSROADS

Muhammad Asad

Qadeem Press

Qadeem Press Edition
Breathing Life into Forgotten Pages
www.qadeempress.com

Find our titles on your favourite online bookstore using the keyword 'Qadeem Press'

DEDICATED
TO
THE MUSLIM YOUTH

CONTENTS

FOREWORD 1

THE OPEN R OAD OF ISLAM 9

THE SPIRIT OF THE WEST 33

THE SHADOW OF THE CRUSADES 63

ABOUT EDUCATION 85

ABOUT IMITATION 103

HADITH AND SUNNAH 113

THE SPIRIT OF THE SUNNAH 133

CONCLUSION 153

COMMENTS 165

THE AUTHOR 167

الحمد لله وحده والصلوة والسلام علی من لا نبی بعده

FOREWORD

Seldom was mankind intellectually as restless as it is in our time. Not only are we faced with a multitude of problems requiring new and unprecedented solutions, but also the angle of vision in which these problems appear before us is different from anything we were accustomed to so far. In all countries society passes through fundamental changes. The pace at which this happens is everywhere different; but everywhere we can observe the same pressing energy which allows of no halt or hesitation.

The world of Islam is no exception in this respect. Here also we see old customs and ideas gradually disappear and new forms emerge. Whereto does this development go ? How deep does it reach ? How far does it fit into the cultural mission of Islam ?

This book has no pretension to giving an exhaustive answer to all these questions. Owing to its limited space only one of the problems facing the Muslims today, namely, the attitude they should adopt towards Western civilization has been selected for discussion. The vast implications of the subject, however, made it necessary to extend our scrutiny over some basic aspects of Islam, more particularly with regard to the principle of *Sunnah*. It was impossible to give here more than the bare outline of a theme wide enough to fill many bulky volumes. But nonetheless—or, perhaps, there fore—I feel confident that this brief sketch will prove, for others, an incentive to further thought on this most important problem.

And now about myself—because the Muslims have a right, when a convert speaks to them, to know how and why he has embraced Islam.

In 1922 I left my native country, Austria, to travel through Africa and Asia as a Special Correspondent to some of the leading Continental newspapers, and spent from that year onward nearly the whole of my time in the Islamic East. My interest in the nations with which I came into contact was in the beginning that of an outsider only. I saw before me a social order and an outlook on life fundamentally different from the European ; and from the very first there grew in me a sympathy for the more tranquil—I should rather say, more human—conception of life, as compared with the hasty, mechanised mode of living in Europe. This sympathy gradually led me to an investigation of the reasons for such a difference, and I became interested in the religious teachings of the Muslims. At the time in question, that interest was not strong enough to draw me into the fold of Islam, but it opened to me a new vista of a progressive human society, organised with a minimum of internal conflicts and a maximum of real brotherly feeling. The reality, however, of present day Muslim life appeared to be very far from the ideal possibilities given in the religious teachings of Islam. Whatever, in Islam, had been progress and movement, had turned, among the Muslims, into indolence and stagnation ; whatever there had been of generosity and readiness for self-sacrifice had become among the present day Muslims, perverted into narrow-mindedness and love of an easy life.

Prompted by the discovery and puzzled by the obvious incongruency between Once and Now, I tried to approach the problem before me from a more intimate point of view : that is, I tried to imagine myself as being *within* the circle of Islam. It was a purely intellectual experiment ; and it revealed to me, within a very short time, the right solution. I realised that the one and only reason for the social and cultural decay of the Muslims consisted in the fact that they had gradually ceased to follow the teachings of Islam in spirit. Islam was still there; but it was a body without soul. The very element which once had stood for the strength of the Muslim world was now responsible for its weakness ; Islamic society had been built, from the very outset, on religious foundations alone, and the weakening of the foundations has necessarily weakened the cultural structure—and possibly might cause its ultimate disappearance.

The more I understood how concrete and how immensely practical the teachings of Islam are, the more eager became my questioning as to why the Muslims had abandoned their full application to real life. I discussed this problem with many thinking Muslims in almost all the countries between the Lybian Desert and the Pamirs, between the Bosphorus and the Arabian Sea. It almost became an obsession which ultimately overshadowed all my other intellectual interests in the world of Islam. The questioning steadily grew in an emphasis—until I, a non-Muslim, talked to Muslims as if I were to defend Islam from their negligence and indolence. The progress was imperceptible to me, until one day— it was in autumn 1925, in the mountains of Afghanistan —a young provincial Governor said to me : "But you are a Muslim, only you don't know it yourself." I was struck by these words and remained silent. But when I came back to Europe once again, in 1926, I saw that the only logical consequence of my attitude was to embrace Islam.

So much about the *circumstances* of my becoming a Muslim. Since then I was asked, time and again : "*Why* did you embrace Islam? What was it that attracted you particularly?—and I must confess : Idon't know of any satisfactory answer. It was not any *particular* teaching that attracted me, but the whole wonderful, inexplicably coherent structure of moral teaching and practical life-programme. I could not say, even now, which aspect of it appeals to me more than any other. Islam appears to me like a perfect work of architecture. All its parts are harmoniously conceived to complement and support each other ; nothing is superfluous and nothing lacking, with the result of an absolute balance and solid composure. Probably this feeling that everything in the teachings and postulates of Islam is "in its proper place" has created the strongest impression on me. There might have been, along with it, other impressions also which today it is difficult for me to analyse. After all, it was a matter of love ; and love is composed of many things : of our desires and our loneliness, of our high aims and our shortcomings, of our strength and our weakness. So it was in my case. Islam came over me like a robber who enters a house by night ; but, unlike a robber, it entered to remain for good.

Ever since then I endeavoured to learn as much as I could about Islam. I studied the Qur'an and the Traditions of the Prophet (peace and blessings be upon him) ; I studied the language of Islam and its history, and a good deal of what has been written about it and against it. I spent over five years in the Hijaz and Najd, mostly in al-Madinah, so that I might experience something of the original surroundings in which this religion was preached by the Arabian Prophet. As the Hijaz is the meeting centre of Muslims from many countries, I was able to compare most of the different religious and social views prevalent in the Islamic world in our days. Those studies and comparisons created in me the firm conviction that Islam, as a spiritual and social phenomenon, is still, in spite of all the drawbacks caused by the deficiencies of the Muslims, by far the greatest driving force mankind has ever experienced ; and all my interest became, since then, centered around the problem of its regeneration.

This little book is a humble contribution towards the great goal. It does not pretend to be a dispassionate survey of affairs ; it is the statement of a case, as I see it : the case of Islam *versus* Western civilization. And it is not written for those with whom Islam is only one of the many, more or less useful, accessories to social life; but rather for those in whose hearts still lives a spark of the flame which burned in the Companions of the Prophet—the flame that once made Islam great as a social order and a cultural achievement.

Delhi, March, 1934. **Muhammad Asad**

THE OPEN ROAD OF ISLAM

One of the slogans most characteristic of the present age is "the conquest of space." Means of communication have been developed which are far beyond the dreams of former generations ; and these new means have set in motion a far more rapid and extensive transfer of goods than ever before within the history of mankind. The result of this development is an economic inter-dependence of nations. No single nation or group can today afford to remain aloof from the rest of the world. Economic development has ceased to be local. Its character has become world-wide. It ignores, at least in its tendency, political boundaries and geographical distances. It carries with itself—and possibly this is even more important than the purely material side of the problem—the ever-increasing necessity of a transfer not only of merchandise but also of thoughts and cultural values. But while those two forces, the economic and the cultural, often go hand in hand, there is a difference in their dynamic rules. The elementary laws of economics require that the exchange of goods between nations be mutual ; this means that no nation can act as buyer only while another nation is always seller in the long run, each of them must play both parts simultaneously, giving to, and taking from, each other, be it directly or through the medium of other actors in the play of economic forces. But in the cultural field this iron rule of exchange is not a necessity, at least not always a visible one, that is to say, the transfer of ideas and cultural influences is not necessarily based on the principle of give-and-take. It lies in human nature that nations and civilizations, which are politically and economically more virile, exert a strong fascination on the weaker or less active communities and influence them in the intellectual and social spheres without being influenced themselves. Such is the situation today with regard to the relations between the Western and the Muslim worlds.

From the view-point of the historical observer the strong, one-sided influence which Western civilization at present exerts on the Muslim world is not at all surprising, because it is the outcome of a long historic process for which there are several analogies elsewhere. But while the historian may be satisfied, for us the problem remains unsettled. For us who are not mere interested spectators, but very real actors in this drama ; for us who regard ourselves as the followers of the Prophet Muhammad (peace and blessings be upon him) the problem in reality begins here. We believe that Islam, unlike other religions, is not only a spiritual attitude of mind, adjustable to different cultural settings, but a self-sufficing orbit of culture and a social system of clearly defined features. When, as is the case today, a foreign civilization extends its radiations into our midst and causes certain changes in our own cultural organism, we are bound to make it clear to ourselves whether that foreign influence runs in the direction of our own cultural possibilities or against them ; whether it acts as an invigorating serum in the body of Islamic culture, or as a poison.

An answer to this question can be found through analysis only. We have to discover the motive forces of both civilizations—the Islamic and that of the modern West—and then to investigate how far a co-operation is possible between them. And as Islamic civilization is essentially a religious one, we must, first of all, try to define the general role of religion in human life.

What we call the "religious attitude" is the natural outcome of man's intellectual and biological constitution. Man is unable to explain to himself the mystery of life, the mystery of birth and death, the mystery of infinity and eternity. His reasoning stops before impregnable walls. He can, therefore, do two things only. The one is, to give up all attempts at understanding life as a *totality*. In this case, man will rely upon the evidence of external experiences alone and will limit his conclusions to their sphere. Thus he will be able to understand single fragments of life, which may increase in number and clarity as rapidly or as slowly as human knowledge of Nature increases, but will, nonetheless, always remain only fragments—the grasp of the totality itself remaining beyond the methodical equipment of human reason. This is the way the natural sciences go. The other possibility—which may well exist side by side with the scientific one—is the way of religion. It leads man, by means of an inner, mostly intuitive, experience, to the acceptance of a unitary explanation of life, generally on the assumption that there exists a supreme Creative Power which governs the Universe according to some pre-conceived plan above and beyond human understanding. As has just been said, this conception does not necessarily preclude man from an investigation of such facts and fragments of life as offer themselves for external observation; there is no inherent antagonism between the external (scientific) and internal (religious) perception. But the latter is, in fact, the only speculative possibility to conceive all life as a unity of essence and motive power ; in short, as a well-balanced, harmonious *totality.* The term "harmonious", though so terribly misused, is very important in this connection, because it implies a corresponding attitude in man himself. The religious man knows that whatever happens to him and within him can never be the result of a blind play of forces without consciousness and purpose ; he believes it to be the outcome of God's conscious will alone, and, therefore, organically integrated with a universal plan. In this way man is enabled to solve the bitter antagonism between the human Self and the objective world of facts and appearances which is called Nature. The human being, with all the intricate mechanism of his soul, with all his desires and fears, his feelings and his speculative uncertainties, sees him self faced by a Nature in which bounty and cruelty, danger and security are mixed in a wondrous, inexplicable way and apparently work on lines entirely different from the methods and the structure of the human mind. Never has purely intellectual philosophy or experimental science been able to solve this conflict. This exactly is the point where religion steps in.

In the light of religious perception and experience, the human, self-conscious Self and the mute, seemingly irresponsible Nature are brought into a relation of spiritual harmony ; because both, the individual consciousness of man and the Nature that surrounds him and is within him, are nothing but coordinate, if different, manifestations of one and the same Creative Will. The immense benefit which religion thus confers upon man is the realisation that he is, and never can cease to be, a well-planned unit in the eternal movement of Creation : a definite part in the infinite organism of universal destiny. The psychological consequence of this conception is a deep feeling of spiritual security-that balance between hopes and fears which distinguishes the positively religious man-whatever his religion—from the irreligious.

This fundamental position is common to all

great religions, whatever their specific doctrines be ; and equally common to all of them is the moral appeal to man to surrender himself to the manifest Will of God. But Islam, and Islam alone, goes beyond this theoretical explanation and exhortation. It not only teaches us that all life is essentially a unity—because it proceeds from the Divine Oneness—but it shows us also the practical way how everyone of us can reproduce, within the limits of his individual, earthly life, the unity of Idea and Action both in his existence and in his consciousness. To attain that supreme goal of life, man is, in Islam, not compelled to renounce the world ; no austerities are required to open a secret door to spiritual purification ; no pressure is exerted upon the mind to believe incomprehensible dogmas in order that salvation be secured. Such things are utterly foreign to Islam : for it is neither a mystical doctrine nor a philosophy. It is simply a programme of life according to the rules of Nature which God has decreed upon His creation ; and its supreme achievement is the complete co-ordination of the spiritual and the material aspects of human life. In the teachings of Islam, both these aspects are not only "reconciled" to each other in the sense of leaving no inherent conflict between the bodily and the moral existence of man, but the fact of their co existence and actual inseparability is insisted upon as the *natural* basis of life.

This, I think, is the reason for the peculiar form of the Islamic prayer in which spiritual concentration and certain bodily movements are co-ordinated with each other. Inimical critics of Islam often select this way of praying as a proof of their allegation that Islam is a religion of formalism and outwardness. And, in fact, people of other religions, who are accustomed neatly to separate the "spiritual" from the "bodily" almost in the same way as the dairyman separates the cream from the milk, cannot easily understand that in the unskimmed milk of Islam both these ingredients, though distinct in their respective constitutions, harmoniously live and express themselves together. In other words, the Islamic prayer consists of mental concentration and bodily movements because human life itself is of such a composition, and because we are supposed to approach God through the sum-total of all the faculties He has bestowed upon us.

A further illustration of this attitude can be seen in the institution of the *Tawaf*, the ceremony of walking round the Ka'bah in Makkah. As it is an indispensable obligation for everyone who enters the Holy City to go seven times round the Ka'bah ; and as the observance of this injunction is one of the three most essential points of the Makkan pilgrimage, we have the right to ask our selves What is the meaning of this ? Is it necessary to express devotion in such a formal way ?

The answer is quite obvious. If we move in a circle around some object we thereby establish that object as the central point of our action. The Ka'bah, towards which every Muslim turns his face in prayer, symbolises the Oneness of God. The bodily movement of the pilgrims in the Tawaf symbolises the activity of human life.

Consequently, the Tawaf implies that not only our devotional thoughts but also our practical life, our actions and endeavours, must have the idea of God and His Oneness for their centre—in accordance with the words of the Holy Qur'ãn.

وما خلقت الجن والانس الاليعبدون (الذّٰريٰت: ٥٦)

"I have not created *Jinn* and Man but that they should worship Me" (Zaryat:56). Thus, the conception of "worship" in Islam is different from that in any other religion. Here it is not restricted to the purely devotional practices, for example, prayers or fasting, but extends over the whole of man's practical life as well. If the object of our life as a whole is to be the worship of God, we necessarily must regard this life, in the totality of all its aspects, as one complex moral responsibility. Thus, all our actions even the seemingly trivial ones, must be performed as acts of worship ; that is, performed *consciously* as constituting a part of God's universal plan. Such a state of things is, for the man of average capability, a distant ideal; but is it not the purpose of religion to bring ideals it no real existence ?

The position of Islam in this respect is unmistakable. It teaches us, firstly, that the permanent worship of God in all the manifold actions of human life is the very meaning of this life ; and, secondly, that the achievement of this purpose remains impossible so long as we divide our life into two parts, the spiritual and the material : they must be bound together, in our consciousness and our action, into one harmonious entity. Our notion of God's Oneness must be reflected in our own striving towards a co-ordination and unification of the various aspects of our life.

A logical consequence of this attitude is a further difference between Islam and all other known religious systems. It is to be found in the fact that Islam, as a teaching, undertakes to define not only the metaphysical relations between man and his Creator but also—and with scarcely less insistence—the earthly relations between the individual and his social surroundings. The worldly life is not regarded as a mere empty shell, as a meaningless shadow of the Hereafter that is to come, but as a self-contained, positive entity. God Himself is a Unity not only in essence but also in purpose ; and therefore, His creation is a Unity, possibly in essence, but certainly in purpose.

Worship of God in the wide sense just explained constitutes, according to Islam, the meaning of human life. And it is this conception alone that shows us the possibility of man's reaching perfection within his individual, earthly life. Of all religious systems, Islam alone declares that individual perfection is possible in our earthly existence. Islam does not postpone this fulfillment until after a suppression of the so-called "bodily" desires, as the Christian teaching does ; nor does Islam promise a continuous chain, of rebirths on a progressively higher plane, as is the case with Hinduism ; nor does Islam agree with Buddhism, according to which perfection and salvation can only be obtained through an annihilation of the individual Self and its emotional links with the world. NO— : Islam is emphatic in the assertion that man can reach perfection in the earthly, individual life and by making full use of all the worldly possibilities of his life.

To avoid misunderstandings, the term "perfection" will have to be defined in the sense it is used here. As long as we have to do with human, biologically limited beings, we cannot possibly consider the idea of "absolute" perfection, because everything absolute belongs to the realm of Divine attributes alone. Human perfection, in its true psychological and moral sense, must necessarily have a relative and purely individual bearing. It does not imply the possession of all imaginable good qualities, nor even the progressive acquisition of new qualities from outside, but solely *the development of the already existing, positive qualities of the individual in such a way as to rouse his innate but otherwise dormant powers.* Owing to the natural variety of the life-phenomena, the inborn qualities of man differ in each individual case. It would be absurd, therefore, to suppose that all human beings should, or even could, strive towards one and the same "type" of perfection—just as it would be absurd to expect a perfect race-horse and a perfect heavy drought horse to possess exactly the same qualities. Both may be individually perfect and satisfactory, but they will be *different*, because their original characters are different. With human beings the case is similar. If perfection were to be standardised in a certain "type"—as Christianity does in the type of the ascetic saint-men would have to give up, or change, or suppress, their individual differentiation. But this would clearly violate the divine law of individual variety which dominates all life on this earth. Therefore Islam, which is not a religion of repression, allows to man a very wide margin in his personal and social existence, so that the various qualities, temperaments and psychological inclinations of different individuals should find their way to positive development according to their individual predisposition. Thus a man may be an ascetic, or he may enjoy the full measure of his sensual possibilities within the lawful limits ; he may be a nomad roaming through the deserts, without food for tomorrow, or a rich merchant surrounded by his goods. As long as he sincerely and consciously submits to the laws decreed by God, he is free to shape his personal life to whatever form his nature directs him. His duty is to make the best of himself so that he might honour the life-gift which his Creator has bestowed upon him ; and to help his fellow-beings, by means of his own development, in their spiritual, social and material endeavours. But the form of his individual life is in no way fixed by a standard. He is free to make his choice from among all the limitless lawful possibilities open to him, The basis of this "liberalism, in Islam, is to be found in the conception that man's original nature is essentially good. Contrary to the Christian idea that man is born sinful, or the teachings of Hinduism, that he is originally low and impure and must painfully stagger through a long chain of transmigrations towards the ultimate goal of Perfection, the Islamic teaching contends that man is born pure and—in the sense explained above—potentially perfect. It is said in the Holy Our'ãn:

لقد خلقنا الانسان فى احسن تقويم (التين: ٤)

"Surely We created man in the best structure"

—but in the same breath the verse continues:

ثم رددناهٔ اسفل سافلين إلا الذين آمنوا وعملوا الصالحات (التين: ٥-٦)

".....and afterwards We reduced him to the lowest of low: with the exception of those who have faith and do good deeds" (surah 95 : 4-6).

In this verse is expressed the doctrine that man is originally good and pure; and, furthermore, that disbelief in God and lack of good actions may destroy his original perfection. On the other hand, man may retain, or regain, that original, individual perfection if he consciously realises God's Oneness and submits to His laws. Thus, according to Islam, evil is never essential or even original; it is an acquisition of man's later life, and is due to a misuse of the innate, positive qualities with which God has endowed every human being. Those qualities are, as has been said before, different in every individual, but always potentially perfect in themselves; and their full development is possible within the period of man's individual life on earth. We take it for granted that the life after death, owing to its entirely changed conditions of feeling and perception, will confer upon us other, quite new, qualities and faculties which will make a still further progress of the human soul possible; but this concerns our future life alone. In this earthly life also, the Islamic teaching definitely asserts, we—everyone of us—can reach a full measure of perfection by developing the positive, already existing traits of which our individualities are composed.

Of all religions, Islam alone makes it possible for man to enjoy the full range of his earthly life without for a moment losing its spiritual orientation. How entirely different is this from the Christian conception! According to the Christian dogma, mankind stumbles under a hereditary sin committed by Adam (Peace be upon him) and Eve, and consequently the whole life is looked upon—

in dogmatic theory at least—as a gloomy dale of sorrows. It is the battlefield of two opposing forces: the evil, represented by *shaitan,* and the good, represented by Jesus Christ. The *shaitan* tries, by means of bodily temptations, to bar the progress of the human soul towards the light eternal ; the soul belongs to Christ, while the body is the playground of *shatanic* influences. One could express it differently: the world of Matter is essentially *shatanic*, while the world of Spirit is divine and good. Everything in human nature that is material, or "carnal," as Christian theology prefers to call it, is a direct result of Adam's succumbing to the advice of the hellish Prince of Darkness and Matter. Therefore, to obtain salvation, man must turn his heart away from this world of the flesh towards the future, spiritual world, where the "sin of mankind" is redeemed by the sacrifice of Christ on the cross.

Even if this dogma is not—and never was—obeyed in practice, the very existence of such a teaching tends to produce a permanent feeling of bad conscience in the religiously inclined man. He is tossed about between the peremptory call to neglect the world and the natural urge of his heart to live and to enjoy this life. The very idea of an unavoidable, because inherited, sin, and of its mystical—to the average intellect incomprehensible—redemption through the suffering of Jesus on the cross, erects a barrier between man's spiritual longing ,and his legitimate desire to live.

In Islam we know nothing of Original Sin; we regard it as incongruent with the idea of God's justice; God does not make the child responsible for the doings of his father: and how could He have made all those numberless generations of mankind responsible for a sin of disobedience committed by a remote ancestor ? It is no doubt possible to construct philosophical explanations of this strange assumption, but for the unsophisticated intellect it will always remain as artificial and as unsatisfactory as the conception of Trinity itself. And as there is no hereditary sin, there is also no universal redemption of mankind in the teachings of Islam.

Redemption and damnation are *individual*. Every Muslim is his own redeemer; he bears all possibilities of spiritual success and failure within his heart. It is said in the Qur'ãn of the human personality:

.....لها ما كسبت وعليها ما اك . ت...(البقر:٢٨٦)

"In its favour is that which it has earned and against it is that which it has become guilty of" (Baqrah: 286). Another verse says:

وان ليس للانسان الاماسعى (النجم: ٣٩)

"Naught shall be reckoned to man but that which he has striven for," (Najam : 39).

But if Islam does not share the gloomy aspect of life as expressed in Christianity, it teaches us, nonetheless, not to attribute to earthly life that exaggerated value which modern Western civilization attributes to it. While the Christian outlook implies that earthly life is a bad business, the modern West—as distinct from Christianity—adores life in exactly the same way as the glutton adores his food: he devours it, but has no respect for it. Islam on the other hand, looks upon earthly life with calm and respect. It does not worship it, but regards it as an organic stage on our way to a higher existence. But just because it is a stage and a necessary stage, too, man has no right to despise or even to underrate the value of his earthly life. Our travel through this world is a necessary positive part in God's plan. Human life, therefore, is of tremendous value; but we must never forget that it is a purely *instrumental* value. In Islam there is no room for the materialistic optimism of the modern West which says : "My Kingdom is of this world alone,"—nor for the life-contempt of the Christian saying : "My Kingdom is not of this world." Islam goes the middle way. The Qur'ãn teaches us to pray:

ربنا آتنا فى الدنيا حسنة وفى الاخرة حسنة
(البقر: ٢٠١)

"Our Lord, give us the good in this world and the good in the Hereafter"! (Baqrah: 201). Thus, the full appreciation of this world and its goods is in no way a handicap for our spiritual endeavours. Material prosperity is desirable, though not a goal in itself. The goal of all our practical activities always ought to be the creation and the maintenance of such personal and social conditions as might be helpful for the development of moral stamina in men. In accordance with this principle, Islam leads man towards a consciousness of moral responsibility in everything he does, whether great or small. The well-known injunction of the Gospels: "Give Caesar that which belongs to Caesar, and give God that which belongs to God"—has no room in the theological structure of Islam, because Islam does not admit the existence of a conflict between the moral and the socio-economic requirements of our existence. In everything there can be only one choice : the choice between Right and Wrong—and nothing in-between. Hence the intense insistence on *action* as an indispensable element of morality.

Every Individual Muslim has to regard himself as personally responsible for all happenings around him, and to strive for the establishment of Right and the abolition of Wrong at every time and in every direction. A sanction for this attitude is to be found in the verse of the Qur'ãn,

كنتم خير امته اخرجت للناس تامرون بالمعروف وتنهون
عن المنكرو تؤمنون بالله (آل عمران: ١١٠)

"You are the best community that has been sent forth unto mankind: You enjoin the Right and forbid the Wrong; and you have faith in God"

(Al-Imran:110).

This is the moral justification of the aggressive activism of Islam, a justification of the early Islamic conquests and of its so-called "imperialism." For Islam was "imperialist," if you insist on this term but this kind of imperialism was not prompted by love of domination, it had nothing to do with economic or national selfishness, nothing with the greed to increase Muslim comforts at other people's cost ; nor has it ever meant the coercion of non-believers into the fold of Islam. It has only meant, as it means today, the construction of a worldly frame for the best possible spiritual development of man. For, according to the teachings of Islam, moral knowledge automatically forces moral responsibility upon man. A mere Platonic discernment between Right and Wrong, without the urge to promote Right and to destroy Wrong, is a gross immorality in itself. In Islam, morality lives and dies with the human endeavour to establish its victory upon earth.

THE SPIRIT OF THE WEST

In the foregoing chapter an attempt has been made to give an outline of the moral foundations of Islam. We "easily realise that Islamic civilization is the most complete form of Theocracy history has ever known. Religious consideration is here above everything and underlies everything. If we compare this attitude with that of Western civilization, we are impressed by the vast difference in outlook.

The modern West is ruled, in its activities and endeavours, by considerations of practical utility and dynamic expansion alone. Its inherent aim is the experimenting with, and the discovery of the potentialities of life, without attributing to this life a moral reality of its own. For the modern European or American the question of meaning and purpose of life has long since lost all its practical importance. Important to him is only the question as to what *forms* life can assume, and as to whether the human race as such is progressing towards ultimate mastership over Nature. This last question the modern Occidental answers in the affirmative, and here he is in agreement with Islam. In the Holy Qur'ãn God says of Adam and his race :

انی جاعل فی الارض خلیفه
(البقره: ۳۰)

"Behold, I am placing a vicegerent on earth"
(Baqrah: 30).

This evidently means that man is destined to rule and to progress on earth. But there is a difference between the Islamic and the Western view-points as to the *quality* of human progress. The modern West believes in the possibility of a progressive spiritual improvement of mankind, in its collective sense, by means of practical achievements and the development of scientific thought. The Islamic view-point, however, is diametrically opposed to this Western, materialistically dynamic conception of humanity.

Islam regards the spiritual possibilities of the collective entity "mankind" as a static quantity : as something that has been definitely laid down in the very constitution of the human nature as such. Islam has never accepted for granted, as the West does, that the human nature—in its general, super-individual sense—is undergoing a process of progressive change and improvement in a similar way as a tree grows : be cause the basis of that nature, the human soul, is not a biological quantity. The fundamental mistake of modern European thought, to regard an increase in material knowledge and comfort as identical with a spiritual and moral *improvement* of mankind, was possible only because of the equally fundamental mistake which consisted in applying biological rules to non-biological facts. At the root of it lies the modern Western unbelief in the existence of what we describe as "soul". Islam, being based on transcendental conceptions, regards the soul as a reality beyond doubt or discussion. Though certainly not opposed to each other, material progress and spiritual progress are not one and the same, relating, as they do, to two distinctly different aspects of human life ; and these two forms of progress do not necessarily depend on one another. They may, but need not always, develop simultaneously.

While clearly admitting the possibility and strongly asserting the desirability of an outward, that is, material progress of mankind as a collective body, Islam as clearly denies the possibility of a spiritual improvement of humanity as a whole by means of its collective achievements. The dynamic element of spiritual improvement is limited to the individual being, and the only possible curve of spiritual and moral development is that between the birth and the death of each single individual. We cannot possibly march towards perfection as a collective body. Everyone must strive towards the spiritual goal as an *individual* and everyone must begin and end with himself.

This decidedly individualistic outlook on the spiritual destinies of man is counter balanced, and indirectly confirmed, by the Islamic rigorous conception of society and social collaboration. The duty of society is to arrange outward life in such a way that the single individual should find as few obstacles as possible, and as much encouragement as possible, in his spiritual endeavours. This is the reason why the Islamic Law, the *shari'ah,* is concerned with human life on its spiritual as well as on its material side, and both with its individual and its social aspects.

Such a conception, as has been said before, is possible only on the basis of a positive belief in the existence of a human soul, and, therefore, in a transcendental purpose of human life. But for the modern Occidental, with his negligent semi-denial of the soul's existence, the question of a purpose of life has no longer any practical importance. He has left all transcendental speculations and considerations behind him.

What we call the religious attitude is always based on the belief that there exists an all-embracing, transcendental moral law, and that we human beings are bound to submit to its commands. But modern Western civilization does not recognise the necessity of man's submission to anything save to economic or social or national requirements. Its real deity is not of a spiritual kind : it is Comfort. And its real, living philosophy is expressed in a Will to Power for power's sake. Both are inherited from the old Roman civilization.

The mention of Roman civilization as— at least to some extent—genetically responsible for the materialism of the modern West may sound strange to those who have heard the frequent comparison of the Roman Empire with the old Islamic Empire. How is such a pronounced difference between the fundamental conception of Islam and the modern West possible if in the past the political expressions of both were akin to one another ? The simple answer is : they were not really akin. That popular, so often quoted comparison, is one of the many historical platitudes with which superficial half science feeds the minds of the present generation. There is nothing whatever in common "between the Islamic and the Roman Empires beyond the fact that both extended over vast territories and heterogeneous peoples—for, during the whole of their existence, these two Empires were directed by utterly different motive-forces and had, so to say, different historical purposes to fulfil. Even on the morphological side we observe a vast difference between the Islamic and the Roman Empires. It took the Roman Empire nearly one thousand years to grow to its full geographic extent and political maturity, while the Islamic Empire sprang up and grew to its fullness within the short period of about eighty years. As regards their respective decay the difference is even more enlightening. The downfall of the Roman Empire, finally sealed by the migrations of the Huns and Goths, was effected during one single century—and was effected so completely that nothing of it remained but works of literature and architecture. The Byzantine Empire, commonly supposed to have been the direct heir of the Roman Empire, was an heir only in so far as it continued to rule over some of the territories which once had formed part of the latter. Its social structure and political organisation had hardly anything to do with the conceptions of Roman polity. The Islamic Empire, on the other hand, as embodied in the Caliphate, underwent, no doubt, many deformations and dynastic changes in the course of its long existence, but its structure remained essentially the same. As to external attacks, even that of the Mongols—which was far more violent than anything the Roman Empire had ever experienced at the hands of the Huns or Goths—was not able to shake the social organisation and the unbroken political existence of the Empire of the Caliphs, though it undoubtedly contributed to the economic and intellectual stagnation of the later times. In contrast with the one century which was needed to destroy the Roman Empire, the Islamic Empire of the Caliphs needed about a millennium of slow decay until its ultimate political breakdown, represented in the extinction of the Ottoman Caliphate, became a fact, followed by the signs of social dissolution which we are witnessing at present.

All this forces the conclusion upon us that the inner strength and social soundness of the Islamic world were superior to any thing mankind has hitherto experienced by way of social organisation. Even Chinese civilization, which has undoubtedly shown similar powers of resistance through many centuries, cannot be used as comparison here. China lies on the edge of a continent, and was until half a century ago—that is, until the rise of modern Japan—beyond the reach of any rival power ; the wars with the Mongols at the time of Changaiz Khan and his successors touched hardly more than the fringe of the Chinese Empire. But the Islamic Empire stretched over three continents and was all the time surrounded by inimical powers of considerable strength and vitality. Since the dawn of history, the so called Near and Middle East was the volcanic centre of conflicting racial and cultural energies ; but the resistance of the Islamic social organisation was, until recently at least, invincible. We need not search far for an explanation of this wonderful spectacle : it was the religious teaching of the Qur'ãn that gave a solid foundation and the life-example of the Prophet Muhammad (peace and blessings be upon him) that became a band of steel around that grand social structure. The Roman

Empire had no such spiritual element to keep it together ; and therefore it broke down so rapidly.

But there is yet a further difference between those two old Empires. While in the Islamic Empire there was no privileged nation, and power was made subservient to the propagation of an idea regarded by its torch-bearers as the sublime religious truth, the idea underlying the Roman Empire was conquest of power and the exploitation of other nations for the benefit of the mother country alone. To promote better living for a privileged group, no violence was for the Romans too bad, no injustice too base. The famous "Roman justice" was justice for the Romans alone. It is clear that such an attitude was possible only on the basis of an entirely materialistic conception of life and civilization—a materialism certainly refined by intellectual taste, but nonetheless foreign to all spiritual values. The Romans never in reality knew religion. Their traditional gods were a pale imitation of Greek mythology, mere colourless ghosts silently accepted for the benefit of social convention. In no way those gods were allowed to interfere with "real" life. When asked, they had to give oracles through the medium of their priests; but they were never supposed to confer moral laws upon men or to direct their actions.

This was the soil out of which modern Western civilization grew. It undoubtedly received many other influences in the course of its development, and it naturally changed and modified the cultural inheritance of Rome in more than one respect. But the fact remains that all that is real today in Western ethics and outlook on life is directly traceable to the old Roman civilization. As the intellectual and social atmosphere of old Rome was utterly utilitarian and anti religious—in fact if not in open admission— so is the atmosphere of the modern West. Without having a proof against transcendental religion, and without even admitting the need of such a proof, modern Western thought, while tolerating and sometimes even emphasising religion as a social convention, generally leaves transcendental ethics out of the range of practical consideration. Western civilization does not strictly *deny* God, but has simply no room and no use for Him in its present intellectual system. It has made a virtue out of an intellectual difficulty of man—his inability to grasp the totality of life. Thus, the modern Occidental is likely to attribute practical importance only to such ideas as lie within the scope of empiric sciences or, at least, are expected to influence men's social relations in a tangible way. And as the question of the existence of God does not *prima facie* belong to either of these two categories, the Western mind is, on principle, inclined to exclude God from the sphere of practical consideration.

The question arises : how is such an attitude compatible with the Christian way of thinking ? Is not Christianity—which is supposed to be spiritual fountain-head of Western civilization—a faith based on transcendental ethics? Of course it is. But, then, there can be no greater error than to consider Western civilization as an outcome of Christianity. The real intellectual foundations of the modern West are to be found in the old Roman conception of life as a purely utilitarian proposition without any transcendental outlook. It can be expressed as follows : "As we do not know anything definite—that is, by means of scientific experiments and calculations—about the origin of human life and its destinies after the bodily death, it is better to concentrate all our energies on the development of our material and intellectual possibilities with out allowing ourselves to be hampered by transcendental ethics and moral postulates based on presumptions which defy scientific proof." There can be no doubt that this attitude, so characteristic of modern Western civilization, is as unacceptable to Christianity as it is to Islam or any other religion, because it is irreligious in its very essence. To ascribe, therefore, the practical achievements of modern Western civilization to the supposed efficacy of Christian teachings, is extremely ridiculous. Christianity has contributed very little to the powerful scientific and material development in which the present civilization of the West excels all others. Indeed, those achievements emerged out of Europe's age-long intellectual fight *against* the Christian Church and its outlook on life.

Through long centuries the spirit of Europe was oppressed by a religious system embodying the contempt of Nature. The note of asceticism which pervades the Gospels from one end to the other, the demand to submit passively to wrong inflicted, the repudiation of sex as something based on the fall of Adam (Peace be upon him) and Eve in the Paradise, the Original Sin and its atonement through Christ's crucifixion—all this leads to an interpretation of human life not as a positive stage but almost as a necessary evil—as an "educative" obstacle on the path of spiritual progress. It is clear that such a belief does not favour energetic endeavours concerning worldly knowledge and the improvement of the conditions of earthly life. And, in deed, for a very long time the intellect of Europe was subdued by this sinister conception of human existence. During the Middle Ages, when the

Church was omnipotent there, Europe had no vitality and no place whatsoever in the realm of scientific research. It lost even all real connection with the philosophical achievements of Rome and Greece out of which European culture had once originated. The intellect revolted more than once ; but it was beaten down by the Church again and again. The history of the Middle Ages is full of that bitter struggle between the genius of Europe and the spirit of the Church.

The liberation of the European mind from the intellectual bondage to which the Christian Church had subjugated it, took place in the time of the Renaissance and was to a very large extent due to the new cultural impulses and ideas which the Arabs had been transmitting to the West for several centuries.

Whatever had been best in the culture of old Greece and the later Hellenistic period, the Arabs had revived in their learning and improved upon in the centuries that followed the establishment of the early Islamic Empire. I do not say that the absorption of Hellenistic thought was an undisputed benefit to the Arabs, and the Muslims generally-because it was not. But for all the difficulties which this revived Hellenistic culture may have caused to the Muslims by introducing Aristotelian and Neo-Platonic philosophy into Islamic theology and jurisprudence, it acted, through the Arabs, as an immense stimulus to Europe. The Middle Ages had laid waste Europe's productive forces. Sciences were stagnant, superstition reigned supreme, the social life was primitive and crude to an extent hardly conceivable today. At that point the cultural influence of the Islamic world—at first through the adventure of the Crusades in the East and the brilliant universities of Muslim Spain in the West, and later through the growing commercial relations established by the republics of Genoa and Venice-began to hammer at the bolted doors of European civilization. Be fore the dazzled eyes of the European scholars and thinkers another civilization appeared—refined, progressive, full of passionate life and in possession of cultural treasures which

Europe had long ago lost and forgotten. What the Arabs had done was far more than a mere revival of old Greece. They had created an entirely new scientific world of their own and developed until then unknown avenues of research and philosophy. All this they communicated through different channels to the Western world : and it is not too much to say that the modern scientific age in which we are living at present was not inaugurated in the cities of Christian Europe, but in such Islamic centres as Damascus, Baghdad, Cairo, Cordova, Nishapur, Samarqand.

The effect of these influences on Europe was tremendous. With the approach of Islamic civilization a new intellectual light dawned on the skies of the West and infused it with fresh life and thirst for progress. It is no more than a just appreciation of its value that European historians term that period of regeneration, the *Renaissance*—that is, "re-birth". It was, in fact, a re-birth of Europe.

The rejuvenating currents emanating from Islamic culture enabled the best minds of Europe to fight with new strength against the disastrous supremacy of the Christian Church. In the beginning this contest had the outward appearance of reform movements which sprang up, almost simultaneously, in different European countries with the object of adapting the Christian way of thinking to the new exigencies of life. These movements were sound in their own way, and, if they had met with real spiritual success, they might have produced a certain reconciliation between science and religious thought in Europe. But, "as it happened, the wrong caused by the Church of the Middle Ages was already too far-reaching to be repaired by mere reformation, which, more over, quickly degenerated into political struggles between interested groups. Instead of being truly reformed, Christianity was merely driven into defence and gradually forced to adopt an apologetic attitude. The Church—whether Catholic or Protestant— did not really give up any of its mental acrobatics, its incomprehensible dogmas, its world-contempt, its unscrupulous support of the powers-that-be at the expense of the oppressed masses of humanity : it merely tried to gloss over these grave failings and to "explain them away" by means of hollow assertions. No wonder, therefore, that, as the decades and the centuries advanced, the hold on religious thought grew weaker and weaker in Europe, until in the 18th century the predominance of the Church was definitely swept overboard by the French Revolution and its cultural consequences in other countries.

At that time again it appeared as if a new spiritual civilization freed from the tyrannical gloom of the scholastic theology of the Middle Ages, had a chance of growth in Europe. In fact, at the end of the 18th and the beginning of the 19th century we encounter some of the best and spiritually most powerful European personalities in the domain of philosophy, art, literature and science. But this spiritual, religious conception of life was and remained restricted to a few individuals. The great European masses, after having been for so long a time imprisoned in religious dogmas which had no connection with the natural endeavours of man, could not, and would not, once those chains were broken, find their way back to a religious orientation.

Perhaps the most important intellectual factor which prevented Europe's religious regeneration was the current conception of Jesus Christ as the Son of God. Philosophically-minded Christians, of course, never took this idea of son ship in its literal sense ; they understood by it a manifestation of God's Mercy in human form. But, unfortunately, not every one has a philosophical mind. For the overwhelming majority of Christians the expression "son" had and has a very direct meaning, although there was always a mystical flavour attached to it. For them, Christ's son ship of God quite naturally led to an anthropomorphisation of God Himself, who assumed the shape of a benignant old man with a white flowing beard: and this shape, perpetuated by innumerable paintings of high artistic value, remained impressed upon the European's subconscious mind. During the time when the dogma of the Church reigned supreme in Europe there was not much inclination to question this strange conception. But with the intellectual shackles of the Middle Ages once broken, the thinking among the Europeans could not reconcile themselves to a humanised God-Father; on the other hand, this anthropomorphisation had become a standing factor in the popular conception of God. After a period of enlightenment, European thinkers instinctively shrank back from the conception of God as presented in the teachings of the Church : and as this was the only conception to which they had been accustomed, they began to reject the very idea of God, and with it, of religion.

In addition to this, the dawn of the industrial era with its glamour of stupendous material progress began to direct men towards new interests, and thus contributed to the subsequent religious vacuum of Europe. In this vacuum the development of Western civilization took a tragic turn-tragic from the viewpoint of anyone who regards religion as the strongest reality in human life. Freed from its former serfdom towards Christianity, the modern European mind overstepped the limit and entrenched itself, by degrees, in a decided antagonism to any form of spiritual claim upon man. Out of the subconscious fear of being once more overwhelmed by forces claiming spiritual authority, Europe became the champion of everything anti-religious in principle and action. It returned to its old Roman heritage.

Thus, one cannot be blamed for the contention that it was not a potential "superiority" of the Christian faith over other creeds which enabled the West to attain its brilliant material achievements for those achievements are unthinkable without the historic struggle of Europe's intellectual forces against the very principles of the Christian Church. Its present materialistic conception of life is Europe's revenge on Christian "spirituality" which had gone astray from the natural truths of life.

It is not within our scope to go deeper into the private relations between Christianity and modern Western civilization. I have only tried to show three of the reasons, perhaps the main reasons, why that civilization is so thoroughly anti-religious in its conceptions and methods : one is the heritage of Roman civilization with its utterly materialistic attitude as regards human life and its inherent value ; another, the revolt of human nature against the Christian world-contempt and the suppression of natural desires and legitimate endeavours of man (followed by the Church's traditional alliance with the holders of political and economic power and its cold-blooded sanction of every exploitation which the power-holders could devise); and, lastly, the anthropomorphic conception of God. This revolt against religion was entirely successful—so successful that the various Christian sects and Churches were gradually compelled to adjust some of their doctrines to the changed social and intellectual conditions of Europe. Instead of influencing and shaping the social life of its adherents, as is the primary duty of religion, Christianity has resigned itself to the role of a tolerated convention and a garb for political enterprises. For the masses it has now only a formal meaning, as was the case with the gods of ancient Rome, which were neither allowed nor supposed to exert any real influence upon society. No doubt, there are still many individuals in the West who feel and think in a religious way and make the most desperate efforts to reconcile their beliefs with the spirit of their civilization—but they are exceptions only. The average Occidental—be he a Democrat or a Fascist, a Capitalist or a Bolshevik, a manual worker or an intellectual—knows only one positive "religion", and that is the worship of material progress, the belief that there is no other goal in life than to make that very life continually easier or, as the current expression goes, "independent of Nature". The temples of this "religion" are the.; gigantic factories, cinemas, chemical laboratories, dancing halls, hydro-electric works : and its priests are bankers, engineers, film stars, captains of industry, record air men. The unavoidable result of this craving after power and pleasure is the creation of hostile groups armed to the teeth and deter mined to destroy each other whenever and wherever their respective interests come to clash. And on the cultural side the result is the creation of a human type whose morality is confined to the question of practical utility alone, and whose highest criterion of good and evil is material success.

In the profound transformation the social life of the West is undergoing at present, that new, utilitarian, morality becomes daily more and more apparent. All virtues having a direct bearing upon the material welfare of society—for example, technical efficiency, patriotism, nationalist group-sense—are being exalted and often absurdly exaggerated in their value : while virtues which, until recently, were valued from a purely ethical point of view, as, for example, filial love or sexual fidelity, rapidly lose their importance—because they do not confer a tangible, material benefit upon society. The age in which the insistence on strong family bonds was decisive for the well-being of the group or the clan is being superseded, in the modern West, by an age of collective organisation, under far wider headlines. And in a society which is essentially technological and is being organised, at a rapidly increasing pace, on purely mechanical lines, the behaviour of a son towards his father is of no great social importance so long as those individuals behave within the limits of general decency imposed by the society on the intercourse between its members. Consequently, the Western father daily loses more and more authority over his son, and quite logically the son loses his respect for the father. Their mutual relations are being slowly overruled and—for all practical purposes—made obsolete by the postulates of a mechanised society which has a tendency to abolish all privileges of one individual over another, and—in the logical development of this idea—also the privileges due to family relationship.

Parallel to this goes the progressive dissolution of the "old" sexual morality. Sexual fidelity and discipline are quickly becoming ; a thing of the past in the modern West, because they were mainly motivated by ethics : and ethical considerations have no tangible, immediate influence on the material well-being of society. And so, discipline in sexual relations is rapidly losing its importance and is being supplanted by the "new" morality which proclaims the unrestricted individual freedom of the human body. In future, the only sexual restriction will be, at the best, derived from considerations of demography and eugenics.

It is not without interest to observe how the anti-religious evolution sketched above has been brought to its logical climax in Soviet Russia, which, on her cultural side, does not represent a development essentially different from the rest of the Western world. On the contrary, it seems that the Communist experiment is nothing else but the culmination and the fulfillment of those decidedly anti-religious and—ultimately— anti-spiritual tendencies of modern Western civilization. It may even be that the present sharp antagonism between the Capitalistic West and Communism is, at its root, due only to the different pace at which those essentially parallel movements are progressing towards their common goal. Their inner similarity will, no doubt, become more and more pronounced in future : but even now it is visible in the fundamental tendency of both Western Capitalism and Communism, to surrender the spiritual individuality of man, and his ethics, to the purely material requirements of a collective machinery called "society", in which the individual is but a cog in a wheel.

The only possible conclusion is, that a civilisation of this kind must be a deadly poison for any culture based on religious values. Our original question, whether it is possible to adapt the Islamic way of thinking and living to the exigencies of Western civilisation, and *vice versa,* must be answered in the negative. In Islam, the first and foremost objective is the moral progress of man, and therefore ethical considerations overrule the purely utilitarian ones. In modern Western civilization the position is exactly reversed. Considerations of material utility dominate all manifestations of human activity, and ethics is being relegated to an obscure background of life and condemned to a merely theoretical existence without the slightest power to influence the community. To talk of ethics, in such circumstances, is nothing short of hypocrisy : and thus the intellectually decent among the modern Western thinkers are subjectively justified if, in their speculations on the social destinies of Western civilization, they avoid any allusion to transcendental ethics. With the less decent—as also with those who are less clearly decided in their moral attitude—the conception of transcendental ethics survives as an irrational factor of thought, much in the same way as the mathematician is obliged to operate with certain "irrational" numbers which represent, in themselves, nothing tangible, but are, nonetheless, required to bridge the gaps of imagination due to the structural limitations of the human mind.

Such an evasive attitude towards ethics is certainly incompatible with a religious orientation: and, therefore, the moral basis of modern Western civilization is incompatible with Islam.

This should in no way preclude the possibility of Muslims receiving from the West certain impulses in the domain of exact and applied sciences ; but their cultural relations should begin and end at that point. To go further and to imitate Western civilization in its spirit, its mode of life and its social organisation is impossible without dealing a fatal blow to the very existence of Islam as a theocratic polity and a practical religion.

THE SHADOW OF THE CRUSADES

Quite apart from spiritual incompatibility, there is one reason more why Muslims should avoid imitating Western civilization : its historical experiences are deeply tinged by a strange animosity against Islam.

To some extent this also is an inheritance from Europe's antiquity. The Greeks and the Romans regarded only themselves as "civilised", while everything foreign, and particularly everything living to the east of the Mediterranean Sea, bore the label "barbarian". Since that time the Occidentals believe that their racial superiority over the rest of mankind is a matter of fact ; and the more or less pronounced contempt of non-European races and nations is one of the standing features of Western civilization.

This alone, however, is not enough to explain its feelings as regards Islam. Here and here alone, the Western attitude is not one of indifferent dislike as in the case of all other "foreign" religions and cultures; it is one of deep-rooted and almost fanatical aversion ; and it is not only intellectual but bears an intensely emotional tint. Europe may not accept the doctrines of Buddhist or Hindu philosophy, but it will always preserve a balanced, reflective attitude of mind with regard to those systems. As soon, however, as it turns towards Islam, the balance is disturbed and an emotional bias creeps in. With very few exceptions, even the most eminent of European orientalists are guilty of an unscientific partiality in their writings on Islam. In their investigations it almost appears as if Islam could not be treated as a mere object of scientific research, but as an accused standing before his judges. Some of these orientalists play the part of a public prosecutor bent on securing a conviction ; others are like a counsel for defence who, being personally convinced that his client is guilty, can only half-heartedly plead for "mitigating circumstances". All in all, the technique of the deductions and conclusions adopted by most of the European orientalists reminds us of the proceedings of those notorious Courts of Inquisition set up by the Catholic Church against its opponents in the Middle Ages : that is to say, they hardly investigate historical facts with an open mind, but start, almost in every case, from a foregone conclusion dictated by prejudice. They select the evidence according to the conclusion they *a priori* intend to reach. Where an arbitrary selection of witnesses is impossible, they cut parts of the evidence of the available ones out of the context, or "interpret" their statements a spirit of unscientific malevolence, without attributing any weight to the presentation of the case by the other party, that is, the Muslims themselves.

The result of such a procedure is the strangely distorted picture of Islam and things Islamic that faces us in the orientalist literature of the West. This distortion is not confined to a particular country it is to be found in England and in Germany, in Russia and in France, in Italy and in Holland—in short, wherever European orientalists turn their eyes on Islam. They seem to be tickled by a sense of malicious pleasure whenever an occasion—real or imaginary—arises for adverse criticism of Islam. And as those European orientalists are not a special race for themselves but only exponents of their civilization and their social surroundings, we necessarily must come to the conclusion that the European mind, on the whole, is for some reason or other prejudiced against Islam as a religion and culture. One of those reasons may be the antique view which divides all the world into "Europeans" and "Barbarians"; and another reason, more directly connected with Islam, can be found by looking back at the past, and particularly at the history of the Middle Ages.

The first great clash between united Europe on the one side and Islam on the other, namely, the Crusades, coincided with the very beginning of European civilization. At that time this civilization, still in alliance with the Church, had just began to see its own way after the dark centuries which had followed the decay of Rome. Its literature was just then passing through a new blossoming. The fine arts were slowly awakening from the lethargy caused by the warlike migrations of the Goths, Huns and Avars. Europe had just emerged out of the crude conditions of the early Middle Ages; it had just acquired a new cultural consciousness and, through it, an increased sensitiveness. And it was exactly at that extremely critical period that the Crusades brought it into a hostile contact with the world of Islam. There had been, to be sure, fights between Muslims and Europeans before the age of the Crusades: the Arab conquests of Sicily and Spain and their attack upon Southern France. But those fights took place before Europe's awakening to its new cultural consciousness, and therefore they had in their time, at least from the European point of view, the character of local issues and were not yet fully understood in all their importance. It was the Crusades, first and foremost, that decided the

European attitude towards Islam for many centuries to come. The Crusades were decisive be cause they fell in the period of Europe's childhood, a period when its peculiar cultural raits were asserting themselves for the first time and were still in the process of moulding. As in individuals, so also in nations the violent impressions of an early childhood persevere, consciously or sub-consciously, throughout the later life. They are so deeply embossed that they can be only with difficulty, and seldom entirely, removed by the intellectual experiences of a later, more reflective and less emotional, age. So it was with the Crusades. They produced one of the deepest and most permanent impressions on Europe's mass psychology. The universal enthusiasm they aroused in their time can be compared with nothing that Europe had experienced ever before and with hardly anything that came afterwards. A wave of intoxication swept over the whole continent, an elation which overstepped, for some time at least, the barriers between states and nations and classes.

It was then for the first time in history that Europe conceived itself as a unity—and it was a unity against the world of Islam. Without indulging in undue exaggerations we can say that *modern Europe was born out of the spirit of the Crusades.* Before that time there existed Anglo-Saxons and Germans, French and Normans, Italians and Danes: but during the Crusades the new concept of "Western civilisation," a cause common to all European nations alike, was created: and it was the hatred of Islam that stood as godfather behind the new creation....

It is one of the great ironies of history that this first act of collective consciousness, the intellectual *constitution*, so to say, of the Western world was due to impulses entirely and unreservedly backed by the Christian Church, whereas the subsequent achievements of the West become possible only through an intellectual revolt against almost everything the Church stood and stands for.

It is a tragic development, both from the viewpoint of the Christian Church and from that of

Islam. Tragic for the Church because it lost after such a startling beginning its hold over the minds of Europe. And tragic for Islam, because it had to bear the fire of the Crusades, in many forms and disguises, through long centuries afterwards.

Out of the unspeakable cruelties, the destruction and the debasement which the pious Knights of the Cross conferred upon the lands of Islam they conquered and subsequently lost, grew the poisonous seed of that age-long animosity which has ever since embittered the relations between East and West. Otherwise, there was no inherent necessity for such a feeling. Though the civilizations of Islam and of the West are entirely different in their spiritual foundations and their social aims, they surely should be able to tolerate one another and to live side by side in a friendly intercourse. This possibility was given not only in theory but in fact. On the Muslim side there always existed a sincere wish for mutual tolerance and respect. When the Caliph Harun ar-Rasheed sent his embassy to Emperor Charlemagne, he was mainly prompted by that desire and not by a wish to profit materially by a friendship with the Franks. Europe was at that time culturally too primitive to appreciate this opportunity to its full extent but it certainly showed no dislike for it. But later on, suddenly, the Crusades appeared on the horizon and destroyed the relations between Islam and the West. Not because they meant war : so many wars between nations have been waged and subsequently forgotten in the course of human history, and so many animosities have turned into friend ship. But the evil the Crusades caused was not restricted to the clang of weapons : it was, first and foremost, an intellectual evil. It consisted in poisoning the European mind against the Muslim world through a deliberate misrepresentation, fostered by the Church, of the teachings and ideals of Islam. It was at the time of the Crusades that the ridiculous notion of Islam as a religion of crude sensualism and brutal violence, of an observance of formalities instead of a purification of the heart, entered the mind of Europe and remained there ; and it was then, for the first time, that the Prophet Muhammad (peace and blessings be upon him) was called in Europe "Mahound".

The seed of hatred was sown. The enthusiasm of the Crusades had soon its sequels elsewhere in Europe : it encouraged the Christians of Spain to fight for the recovery of that country from the "yoke of the heathens". The destruction of Muslim Spain took centuries to be accomplished. But precisely for the reason of the long duration of this fight, the anti-Islamic feeling of Europe deepened and grew to permanency. It resulted in the extermination of the Muslim element in Spain after the most ferocious and merciless persecution the world had ever witnessed, and that victory was echoed by the rejoicings of all Europe—although its after-effect was the destruction of a most glorious culture and its supersession by medieval ignorance and crudeness.

Before the echo of the events on Spain had time to die away, a third event of great importance marred the relations between the Western world and Islam : the fall of Constantinople into the hands of the Turks. In the eyes of Europe there had been still something of the old Greek and Roman glamour left over Byzantium, and it had "been regarded as Europe's bulwark against the "barbarians" of Asia. With its ultimate fall the gateway of Europe was thrown open to the Muslim flood. In the warlike centuries that followed, the hostility of Europe against Islam became a matter not only of cultural but also of political importance; and this contributed to its intensity.

With all this, Europe considerably profited by these conflicts. The Renaissance, the revival of European arts and sciences with its extensive borrowing from Islamić, mainly Arabic, sources, was largely due to the material contact between East and West. Europe gained by it, in the domain of culture, far more than the world of Islam ever did ; but it never acknowledged this eternal indebtedness to the Muslims by a diminution of its old hatred of Islam. On the contrary, that hatred grew with the progress of the time and hardened into a custom. It overshadowed the popular feeling whenever the word "Muslim" was mentioned, it entered the realm of popular proverbs, it was hammered into the heart of every European man and woman. And what was most remarkable, it outlived all cultural changes. The time of the Reformation came, when religious factions divided Europe and sect stood in arms against sect ; but the hatred of Islam was common to all of them. A time came when religious feeling began to vanish in Europe : but the hatred of Islam remained. It is a most characteristic fact that the great French philosopher and poet, Voltaire, one of the most vigorous enemies of Christianity and its Church in the 18th century, was at the same time a fanatical hater of Islam and its Prophet. Some decades later there came a time when learned men in the West began to study foreign cultures and to approach them sympathetically : but in the case of Islam the traditional scorn crept as an irrational bias into their scientific investigations, and the cultural gulf which history had unfortunately laid between Europe and the world of Islam remained unbridged.

The contempt of Islam had become part and parcel of European thought. It is true that the first orientalists in modern times were Christian missionaries working in Muslim countries, and the distorted pictures they drew from the teachings and the history of Islam were calculated to influence the Europeans in their attitude towards the "heathens" but this twist of mind perseveres even new, when the orientalist sciences have long since become emancipated from missionary influences, and have no more a misguided religious zeal for an excuse. Their prejudice against Islam is simply an atavistic instinct, an idiosyncrasy based on the impression which the Crusades, with all their sequels, caused on the mind of early Europe.

One could well ask : How does it happen that such an old resentment, religious in its origin and possible in its time because of the spiritual predominance of the Christian Church, still perseveres in Europe at a time when the religious feeling there is undoubtedly a matter of the past ?

But to a psychologist such entanglements are not at all astonishing. He knows now perfectly well that a person may completely lose the religious beliefs which were imparted to him during his childhood, while some peculiar superstition, originally connected with those now discarded beliefs, remains in force and defies all rational explanation throughout the whole life of that person. Such is the case with the European attitude towards Islam. Though the religious feeling which was at the root of the anti-Islamic resentment has in the meantime given way to a more materialistic outlook on life, that old resentment itself remains as a subconscious factor in the mind of Europe. The degree of its strength varies, of course, in each individual case, but its existence cannot be disputed. The spirit of the Crusades—in a very diluted form, to be sure—still lingers over Europe, and the attitude of its civilization towards the Muslim world bears distinct traces of that diehard ghost.

In Muslim circles we often hear the assertion that Europe's hatred of Islam, due to those violent conflicts in the past, is gradually disappearing in our days. It is even alleged that Europe shows signs of *inclination* towards Islam as a religious and social teaching, and many Muslims quite seriously believe that wholesale conversions of Europeans to Islam are imminent. This belief is not unreasonable for us who hold that of all religious systems, Islam alone can successfully stand the test of unbiased criticism. We were, moreover, told by the Prophet that ultimately Islam would be accepted by all mankind. But, on the other hand, there is not the slightest evidence that this •could happen within the conceivable future. So far as Western civilization is concerned, this can possibly happen after a series of terrible social and mental cataclysms which would shatter the present cultural self-conceit of Europe and change its mentality so as to make it apt and ready to accept a religious explanation of life. Today the Western world is still completely lost in the adoration of its material achievements and in the belief that comfort, and comfort alone, is a goal worth striving for. Its materialism, its denunciation of a religious orientation of thought are certainly increasing in force, and not decreasing, as some optimistic Muslim observers would wish us to believe.

It is said that modern science begins to admit the existence of a uniform creative power behind the visible framework of Nature ; and this, those optimists allege, is the dawn of a new religious consciousness in the Western world. But this assumption betrays only a misunderstanding of European scientific thought. No serious scientist can or ever could deny the probability of the universe being due, in its origin, to some single, dynamic cause. The question, however, is, and always was, as to the qualities which one could attribute to that "cause". All transcendental religious systems assert that it is a power possessing absolute consciousness and insight, a power which creates and rules the universe according to some plan and purpose, without being itself limited by any law; in one world; it is God. But modern science as such is neither prepared nor inclined to go so far (in fact, this is not the domain of science) and leaves the question of the consciousness and independence —in other words, the divinity—of that creative power quite open. Its attitude is some thing like this : "It might be, but I don't know it and have no scientific means to know". In future this philosophy may perhaps develop into some sort of pantheistic agnosticism in which soul and matter, purpose and existence, creator and created are one and the same. It is difficult to admit that such a belief could be regarded as a step forward towards the positive, Islamic conception of God : for it is not a farewell to materialism but simply its elevation to a higher, more refined intellectual level.

As a matter of fact, Europe was never farther from Islam than it is today. Its active hostility against our religion may be on the decline; this, however, is not due to an appreciation of the Islamic teachings but to the growing cultural weakness and disintegration of the Islamic world. Europe was once afraid of Islam, and this fear forced it to adopt an inimical attitude towards every thing that had Islamic colour, even to purely spiritual and social matters. But at a time when Islam has lost most of its importance as a factor opposed to European political interests, it is quite natural that with the diminished fear Europe should also lose some of the original intensity of its anti-Islamic feelings. If these have become less pronounced and active, this does not entitle us to the conclusion that West has inwardly come nearer to Islam; it only indicates its growing indifference towards Islam.

By no means has Western civilization changed its peculiar mental attitude. It is at present as strongly opposed to a religious conception of life as it was ever before ; and, as I have said, there is no convincing evidence that a change is likely to take place in the near future. The existence of Islamic missions in the West and the fact that some Europeans and Americans have embraced Islam (in most cases without fully under-standing its teachings) is no argument at all. In a period in which materialism is triumphant on the whole line, it is only natural that a few individuals here and there who have still a longing for spiritual regeneration, eagerly listen to any creed based on religious conceptions. In this respect Muslim missions do not stand alone in the West. There are numberless Christian mystical sects with "revivalist" tendencies, there is the fairly strong Theosophic movement, there are Buddhist temples and missions and converts in various European cities. Using exactly the same arguments as the Muslim missions use, those Buddhist missions could claim (and do claim) that Europe is "coming nearer" to Buddhism. In both cases the assertion is ridiculous. The conversion of a few individuals to Buddhism or Islam does not in the least prove that either of the two creeds has really begun to influence Western life on an appreciable scale. One could go even further and say that none of those missions has been able to arouse more than a very moderate curiosity mainly due to the fascination which an "exotic" creed exerts upon the minds of romantically inclined people. Certainly there are exceptions, and some of the converts may be earnest seekers after truth ; but exceptions are not enough to change the aspect of a civilization. On the other hand, if we compare the number of those exceptional conversions with the number of the Occidentals who are daily flocking into the ranks of purely materialistic social creeds, as Marxism or Fascism, we are able to appreciate more correctly the trend of modern Western civilization.

It may be, as has been pointed out be fore, that the growing social and economic unrest, and possibly also a new series of world wars of hitherto unknown dimensions and scientific terrors will lead the materialist self-conceit of Western civilization in such a gruesome way *ad absurdum,* that its people will begin once more, in humility and earnest, to search after spiritual truths : and then a successful preaching of Islam in the West might become possible. But such a change is still hidden behind the horizon of the future. It is a dangerous, self-deceiving optimism, therefore, for Muslims to talk of Islamic influences as being on their way to conquer the spirit of Europe. Such a talk is in reality nothing but the old Mahdi belief in a "rationalist" disguise—the belief in a power that would suddenly appear and make the tottering structure of Islam triumphant on earth. This belief is dangerous, because it is pleasant and easy and tends to swindle ourselves away from the realisation of the fact that we are culturally nowhere, while Western influences are today most potent in the Muslim world ; that we are sleeping, while those influences undermine and destroy Islamic society everywhere. To desire the expansion of Islam is one thing ; and to build false hopes on this desire is another.

We are dreaming of the Light of Islam spreading over the lands far away ; while the youth of Islam, in our immediate surroundings, is deserting our cause and our hope.

ABOUT EDUCATION

So long as Muslims continue looking towards Western civilization as the only force that could regenerate their own stagnant civilization, they destroy their self-confidence and, indirectly, support the Western assertion that Islam is a "spent force".

In the previous chapters some reasons have been given for the opinion that Islam and Western civilization, being built on diametrically opposed conceptions of life, are not compatible in spirit. This being so, how could we expect that the education of Muslim youth on Western lines, an education based entirely on European cultural experiences and values, would remain free from anti-Islamic influences?

We are not justified to expect this. Except in rare cases, where a particularly brilliant mind may triumph over the educational matter, Western education of Muslim youth is bound to undermine their will, believe in the message of the Prophet, their will to regard themselves as representatives of the peculiar theocratic civilization of Islam. There can be no doubt whatever that religious belief is rapidly losing ground among the "intelligentsia" educated on Western lines. This, of course, does not imply that Islam has preserved its integrity as a practical religion among the non-educated classes; but there, anyhow, we generally find a far greater sentimental response to the call of Islam—in the primitive way they understand it—than among the Westernised "intelligentsia". The explanation of this estrangement is not that the Western science with which they have been fed has furnished any reasonable argument against the truth of our religious teachings, but that the intellectual atmosphere of modern Western civilization is so intensely anti-religious that it imposes itself as a dead weight upon the religious potentialities of the young Muslim generation.

Religious belief and unbelief are very rarely a matter of argument alone. In some cases the one or the other is gained by way of intuition or, let us say, insight. But mostly it is communicated to man by his cultural surroundings. Think of a child who from his earliest days is systematically trained to hear perfectly rendered musical tunes. His ear grows accustomed to discern tone, rhythm and harmony; and in his later age he will be able, if not to produce and to render, at least to understand the most difficult music. But a child, who during the whole of his early life never heard anything resembling music, would afterwards find it hard to appreciate even its elements. It is the same with religious associations. As there possibly are some individuals to whom nature has completely denied an "ear" for music, so—possibly but not probably—there are individuals who are perfectly "deaf" to the voice of religion. But for the over whelming number of normal human beings the alternative between religious belief and unbelief is decided by the atmosphere in which they are brought up. Therefore the Prophet said

ما من مولود الا يولد علے الفطره فابواه يهودانه اوينصرانه
اويمجسانه (صحيح البخارى)

"Every child is born in natural purity it is his parents who make him a Jew, a Christian, or an idol-worshipper" (*Sahih ul-Bukhari*).

The term "parents" used in the above *Hadith* can logically be extended to the general environment—family life, school, society, etc.—by which the early development of the child as determined. It cannot be denied that in the present state of decadence the religious atmosphere in many Muslim houses is of such a low and intellectually degraded type that it may produce in the growing youth the first incentive to turn his back on religion. This surely may be so; but in the case of the education of young Muslims on Western lines the effect not only may be, but most probably will be, an anti-religious attitude in later life.

But here comes the great question : what should be our attitude towards modern learning ?

A protest against Western education of Muslims does not in the least mean that Islam could be opposed to education as such. This allegation of our opponents has neither a theological nor an historical foundation. The Holy Qur'ãn is full of expressions like : "that you may become wise", "that you may think", "that you may know". It is said at the beginning of the Holy Book

وعلم آدم الاسماء كلها (البقر: ٣١)

"And He (God) taught Adam all the names' (*Baqrah:* 31)—and the subsequent verses show that owing to his knowledge of those "names" man is, in a certain respect, superior even to the angels. The "names" are a symbolic expression for the power of defining terms, the power of articulated thinking which is peculiar to the human being, and which enables him, in the words of the Qur'ãn, to be God's vicegerent on earth. And if order to make a systematic use of his thinking, man must *learn* and therefore the Prophet (peace and blessings be upon him) said

من سلک طریقا یلتمس فیه علما سهل اللّٰه له به طریقا
الی الجنة (صحیح مسلم)

"If anybody goes on his way in search of knowledge, God will make easy for him the way to Paradise" *(Sahih Muslim)*.

ان فضل العالم علی العابد کفضل القمر لیلة البدر علی
سائر الکواکب (ترمذی، ابوداؤد، ابن ماجه)

"The superiority of the learned man over a (mere) worshipper is like the superiority of the moon on a night when it is full over all other stars" *(Musnad Ibn Hanbal, Jami at-Tirmidhi, Sunan Abu Da'ud, Sunan Ibn Majah, Sunan ad-Darimi)*.

But it is not even necessary to quote verses of the Qur'ãn or sayings of the Prophet in defence of the Islamic attitude towards learning. History proves beyond any possibility of doubt that no religion has ever given a stimulus to scientific progress similar to that of Islam. The encouragement which learning and scientific research received from Islamic theology resulted in the splendid cultural achievements in the days of the Umayyads and Abbassides and the Arab rule in Spain. Europe should known this well, for its own culture owes to Islam no thing less than the Renaissance ("re-birth") after centuries of darkness. I do not mention this in order that we might pride our selves in those glorious memories at a time when the Islamic world has forsaken its own tradition and reverted into blindness and intellectual poverty. We have no right, in our present misery, to boast of past glories. But we must realise that it was the negligence of Muslim and not any deficiency in the Islamic teaching which caused our present decay.

Islam was never a barrier to progress and science. It appreciates the intellectual activities of man to such a degree as to place him above the angels. No other religion went over so far in asserting the dominance of reason and, consequently, of learning, above all other manifestations of life. If we conform ourselves to the principles of this religion we cannot wish to eliminate modern learning from our life. We must have the wish to learn and to progress and to become scientifically and economically as efficient as the Western nations are. But the one thing Muslims must not wish is to see with Western eyes, think in Western thoughts: they must not wish, if they desire to remain Muslim, to exchange the spiritual civilization of Islam for the materialistic experiments of the West.

Knowledge itself is neither Western nor Eastern; it is universal—just as natural facts are universal. But the angle of vision from which facts can be regarded and presented varies with the cultural temperaments of the nations. Biology as such, or physics, or botany, are neither materialistic nor spiritual in their' scope and purpose; they are concerned with the observation, collection and definition and facts and the derivation from them of general rules. But the inductive, philosophical conclusion we derive from these sciences—are not based on facts and observations alone but are influenced, to a very large extent, by our pre existing temperamental or intuitive attitude towards life and its problems. The great German philosopher Kant, remarks: "It seems surprising at first, but is nonetheless certain, that our reason does not draw its conclusions from Nature, but prescribes them *to* it." In short, it is only the subjective angle of vision that matters here; for it may change entirely our interpretation of the object. Thus science, which is neither materialistic nor spiritual in itself, may lead us to highly divergent interpretations of the Universe: interpretations, that is, which may be spiritual or materialistic according to our own predisposition. The West, not withstanding its highly refined intellectualism, is materialistically predisposed and, therefore, anti-religious in its conception and fundamental presumption; and so must be the Western educational system as a whole. In other words, not the study of modern, empiric sciences is detrimental to the cultural reality of Islam, but the spirit of Western civilization through which Muslims approach those sciences.

It is very unfortunate that our own age-long indifference and negligence, so far as scientific research is concerned, have made us entirely dependent on Occidental sources of learning. If we had always followed that principle of Islam which imposes the duty of learning and knowledge on every Muslim, we would not have to look today for modern sciences towards the Occidental in the same way as a man dying of thirst in the desert looks towards the mirage of water on the horizon. But as the Muslims had neglected their own possibilities for a long time, they have fallen into ignorance and poverty, while Europe took a mighty step forward. It will take long to bridge this difference. Until then we naturally will be obliged to accept modern sciences through the educational media of the West. But this only means that we are bound to accept the scientific matter and method, and nothing else. In other words, we should not hesitate to study exact sciences on Western lines, but we should not concede to their philosophy any part in the education of Muslim youth. Of course, one could say that at present many of the exact sciences, for example, atomic physics, have gone beyond purely empirical investigation and have entered philosophical domains ; and that it is in many cases extremely difficult to draw any distinct line between empirical science and speculative philosophy. This is true. But, on the other hand, this exactly is the point where Islamic culture will have to reassert itself. It will be the duty and the opportunity of Muslim scientists, when once they reach those border-lines of scientific investigation, to apply their powers of speculative reasoning independently of Western philosophical theories. Out of their own—Islamic-attitude they probably will arrive at conclusions different from those of the majority of the modern Western scientists.

But whatever future may bring, it is decidedly possible, even today, to study and to teach science without a slavish submission to the intellectual attitude of the West. The thing the world of Islam urgently needs today is not a new philosophical outlook, but only an up-to-date scientific and technical equipment.

If I were to make proposals to an ideal Educational Board governed by Islamic considerations alone, I would urge that of all intellectual achievements of the West only natural sciences (in the above-mentioned, reserved attitude) and mathematics should be taught in Muslims schools, while the tuition of European philosophy, literature and history should lose the position of primacy which today it holds in the curriculum. Our attitude towards European philosophy should he clear from the foregoing. And as to European literature, it certainly should not be overlooked—but it should be relegated to its proper, philological position. The way it is at present taught in Muslim countries is frankly biased. The boundless exaggeration of its values naturally induces young and unripe minds to imbibe whole-heartedly the spirit of Western civilization before its negative aspects can be sufficiently appreciated. And so the ground is prepared not only for a Platonic adoration but also for a practical imitation of Western civilization—which can never go together with the spirit of Islam. The present role of European literature in Muslim schools should be taken over by a reasonable, discriminating tuition of Islamic literature with a view to impress the student with the depth and richness of Islamic culture, and thus to infuse into him a new hope for its future.

If the tuition of European literature, in the form it is prevalent today in many Muslim institutions, contributes to the estrangement of young Muslims from Islam, the same, in a far larger measure, is true of the European interpretation of world-history. In it the old attitude "Roman *versus* Barbarians" very distinctly comes to its own. Their presentation of history aims—without admitting the aim—at proving that the Western races and their civilization are superior to anything that has or could be produced in this world ; and so it gives a sort of moral justification to the Western quest of domination over the rest of the world. From the time of the Romans, the European nations are accustomed to regard all differences between East and West from the standpoint of a presumed European "norm". Their reasoning works on the presumption that the development of humanity can be judged only on the basis of European cultural experiences. Such a narrowed angle of vision necessarily produces a distorted perspective, and the farther the lines of observation recede from the habitual basis of the European outlook, the more difficult it becomes for Europeans to grasp the real appearance and the structure of the historical objects under consideration.

Owing to this ego-centric attitude of the Europeans, their descriptive history of the world was, until very recently at least, in reality nothing but an enlarged history of the West. The non-European nations were taken into account only in so far as their existence and development had any direct influence on the destinies of Europe. But if you depict the history of European nations in great detail and in vivid colours and allow only here and there side-glimpses at the remaining parts of the world, the reader is prone to succumb to the illusion that the greatness of the European achievement in social and intellectual respects is out of all proportion to that of the rest of the world. Thus it almost appears as if the world had been created for the sake of Europe and its civilizations alone, while all other civilization were meant only to form an appropriate setting for all that Western glory. The only effect such historical training can have upon the minds of young non-European peoples is a feeling of inferiority in so far as their own culture, their own historic past and their own future possibilities are concerned. They are systematically trained to disdain their own future—unless it be a future surrender to Western ideals.

In order to counteract these evil effects, the responsible leaders of Islamic thought should do their utmost to revise the tuition of history in Muslim institutions. This is a difficult task, no doubt, and it will require a thorough overhaul of our historical training before a new history of the world, as seen with Muslim eyes, is produced. But if the task is difficult it is none the less possible and, moreover, imperative. Otherwise our younger generation will continue to be fed with undercurrents of a contempt for Islam; and the result will be a deepening of its inferiority complex. This inferiority complex could no doubt be overcome if the Muslims were prepared to assimilate Western culture in its entirety and to banish Islam from their life. But are they prepared to do that?

We believe, and the recent development of the West reaffirms this belief, that the ethics of Islam, its concepts of social and personal morality of justice, of liberty, are infinitely higher, infinitely more perfect than the corresponding concepts and ideas within Western civilization. Islam has abolished racial hatred and opened the way for human brotherhood and equality; but Western civilization is still unable to look beyond the narrow horizon of racial and national antagonisms. Islam has never known classes and class warfare within its society ; but the whole of European history, from the days of Greece and Rome down to our time, is full of class struggle and social hatred. Again and again it must be repeated that there is one thing only which a Muslim can profitably learn from the West, namely, the exact sciences in their pure and applied forms. This necessity for a quest of science from outside should not induce a Muslim to consider Western civilization as superior to his own—or else he does not understand what Islam stands for. The superiority of one culture or civilization over another does not consist in the possession of a greater amount of material knowledge (although the latter is most desirable), but in its ethical energy, in its greater possibility to explain and to co-ordinate all aspects of human life. And in this respect Islam surpasses every other culture. We have only to follow its rules in order to achieve the utmost human beings are capable of achieving. But we cannot and must not imitate Western civilization if we wish to preserve and to revive the values of Islam. The evil which the intellectual influence of that civilization causes in the body of Islam is far greater than the material profit it possibly could confer.

If Muslims were negligent, in the past, of scientific research, they cannot hope to repair that mistake today by an unrestricted acceptance of Western learning. All our scientific backwardness and our poverty stand no comparison whatever with the deadly effect which our blind following of the Western educational structure would have on the religious possibilities of the Muslim world. If we wish to preserve the reality of Islam as a cultural factor, we must guard against the intellectual atmosphere of Western civilization which is about to conquer our society and our inclinations. By imitating the manners and the mode of life of the West, the Muslims are being gradually forced to adopt the Western outlook: for the imitation of outward appearance leads, by degrees, to a corresponding assimilation of the world-view responsible for that appearance.

ABOUT IMITATION

The imitation—individually and socially —of the Western mode of life by Muslims is undoubtedly the greatest danger for the existence—or rather the revival—of Islamic civilization. The origin of this cultural malady (it is hardly possible to call it otherwise) dates several decades back and is connected with the despair of Muslims who saw the material power and progress of the West and entrusted it with the deplorable state of their own society. Out of Muslim ignorance of the true teachings of Islam— very largely due to the narrow-minded attitude of the so-called '*ulama*' class—arose the idea that Muslims might not be able to keep pace with the progress of the rest of the world unless they adopted the social and economic rules of the West. The Muslim world was stagnant : and many Muslims came to the very superficial conclusion that the Islamic system of society and economics is not agreeable with the requirements of progress, and should, therefore, be modified on Western lines. Those "enlightened" people did not trouble to inquire how far Islam, as a teaching, was responsible for the decadence of Muslims: they did not stop to investigate the real attitude of Islam, that is, of Qur'ãn and *Sunnah* ; they merely pointed out that the teachings of their contemporary theologians were in most of the cases an obstacle to progress and material achievement. Instead of turning their attention to the original sources of Islam, they silently identified the *Shari'ah* with the purified *fiqah* of the present days, and found the latter wanting in many respects; subsequently, they lost all practical interest in the *Shari'ah* and relegated it to the realm of history and book knowledge. And so an imitation of Western civilization appeared to them as the only outlet from the mire of the Muslim degeneration.

The more thoughtful works of recent times—among them the splendid book *Islamlashmaq* by

Prince Sa'id Haleem Pasha, which conclusively proved that the Islamic *Shari'ah* is not the hindrance to modern progress that it recently was thought to be— came too late to stem the tide of blind admiration of the West by so many Muslims. The healing effect of those works was neutralised by a flood of second-rate apologetic literature which—while not openly disclaiming the practical teachings of Islam—tried to show that the *Shari'ah* could well be subordinated to the social and economic conceptions of the Western world. The imitation of Western civilization by Muslims was thus seemingly justified and the way was paved to that gradual renunciation of the most elementary social principles of Islam—always under the guise of Islamic "progress"— which today marks the evolution of several of the most advanced Muslim countries.

It is futile to argue, as many of the Muslim "intelligentsia" do, that it is of no spiritual consequence whatsoever whether we live in this or that way, whether we put on European or our fathers' dress, whether we are conservative in our customs or not. Of course, there is no narrow-mindedness in Islam. As has been said in the first chapter, Islam concedes to man a very wide range of possibilities so long as he does not act in contradiction to religious commands. But quite apart from the fact that many a thing which is an essential part of the Western social structure—as, for example, the free intermingling of the sexes, or interest on capital as a basis of economic activity—is unmistakably opposed to the teachings of Islam, the innate character of Western civilization definitely precludes, as I have tried to show, a religious orientation in man. And only very superficial people can believe that it is possible to imitate a civilization in its external appearance without being at the same time affected by its spirit. A civilization is not an empty form, but a living energy. The moment we begin to accept the form, its inherent currents and dynamic influences set to work in ourselves and mould slowly, imperceptibly, our while mental attitude.

It is in perfect appreciation of this experience that the Prophet said:

من تشبه بقوم فهومنهم (سنن ابوداؤد)

"Whose imitates other people becomes one of them *(Musnad Ibn Hanbal, Sunan Abi Da'ud)*.

This well-known *Hadith* is not only a moral hint but also an objective statement which lays down the inevitability of Muslims being assimilated by any non-Muslim civilization they imitate in its external appearance.

In this respect it is hardly possible to see a fundamental difference between "important" and "unimportant" aspects of social life. Nothing is unimportant in this context. There can be no greater mistake than to suppose that dress, for example, is something purely "external" and thus of no consequence to the intellectual and spiritual Self of man. Dress is generally the outcome of an age-long development of a people's taste in a particular direction. Its fashion corresponds to the aesthetic conception of that people, and so to its inclinations. It has been shaped and is being constantly re-shaped according to the change through which the character and the inclinations of its people are passing. European fashion of today, for instance, thoroughly corresponds to the intellectual and moral character of Europe. While wearing European dress, the Muslim unconsciously adapts his taste to that of Europe and twists his own intellectual and moral Self in such a way that ultimately fits the new dress. And in doing so he renounces the cultural possibilities of his own people ; he renounces their traditional tastes, their aesthetic valuations, their likes and dislikes, and accepts the livery of intellectual and moral serfdom which a foreign civilization has conferred upon him.

If a Muslim imitates the dress, the manners and the mode of life of Europe, he betrays his preference for European civilization, whatever else his avowed pretensions be. It is practically impossible to imitate a foreign civilization in its intellectual and aesthetic design without appreciating its spirit. And it is equally impossible to appreciate the spirit of a civilization which is opposed to a religious outlook on life—and yet to remain a good Muslim.

The tendency to imitate a foreign civilization is the outcome of a feeling of inferiority. This, and nothing else, is the matter with the Muslims who imitate Western civilization. They contrast its power and technical skill and brilliant surface with the sad misery of the world of Islam: and they begin to believe that in our time there is no way but the Western way. To blame Islam for our own shortcomings is the fashion of the day. At the best, our so-called intellectuals adopt an apologetic attitude and try to convince themselves and others that Islam is compatible with Western civilization.

In order to achieve the regeneration of Islam, the Muslims must, before adopting any measures of reform, free themselves entirely from the spirit of apology for their religion. A Muslim must live with his head lifted up. He must realise that he is distinct and different from the rest of the world, and he must learn to be proud of his being different.

He should endeavour to *preserve* this difference as a precious quality, and pronounce it boldly to the world—instead of apologising for it and trying to merge into other cultural circles. This does not mean that Muslims should seclude themselves from the voices coming from without. One may always receive new positive influences from a foreign civilization without necessarily destroying his own. An example of this kind was the European Renaissance. There we have seen how readily Europe accepted Arab influence in the matter and method of learning. But it never imitated the outward appearance and the spirit of Arabian culture, and never sacrificed its own intellectual and aesthetic independence. It used the Arab influences only as a fertiliser upon its own soil, just as the Arabs had used Hellenistic influences in their time. In both cases, the result was a strong, new growth of an indigenous civilization, full of self-confidence and pride in itself. No civilization can prosper, or even exist, after having lost this pride and the connection with its own past.

But the world of Islam, with its growing tendency to imitate Europe and to assimilate Western ideas and ideals, is gradually cutting away the bonds which link it with its past, and is losing therefore not only its cultural but also its spiritual ground. It resembles a tree that was strong as long as it was deeply rooted in the soil. But the mountain torrent of Western civilization has washed those roots bare: and the tree slowly decays for want of nourishment. Its leaves fall, its branches wither away. At the end the trunk itself stands in danger of collapsing.

Western civilization, then, cannot be the right means of reviving the Islamic world from the mental and social stupor caused by the degeneration of practical religion into a mere custom without life and moral urge in it. Where else, then, should Muslims look for the spiritual and intellectual impetus so badly needed in these days?

The answer is as simple as the question; indeed, it is already contained in the question. Islam, as has been pointed out many times before, is not only a "belief of heart" but also a very clearly defined programme of individual and social life. It can be destroyed by being assimilated to a foreign culture which has essentially different moral foundations. Equally, it can be regenerated the moment it is brought back to its own reality and given the value of a factor determining and shaping our personal and social existence in all its aspects.

Under the impact of new ideas and conflicting cultural currents, so characteristic of the period in which we are living, Islam can no longer afford to remain an empty form. Its magic sleep of centuries is broken; it has to rise or to die. The problem facing the Muslims today is the problem of the traveller who has come to crossroads. He can remain standing where he is; but that would mean death of starvation. He can choose the road bearing the sign "Towards Western Civilization" ; but then he would have to say good-bye to his past for ever. Or he can choose the other road, the one over which is written: "Towards the Reality of Islam". It is this road alone which can appeal to those who believe in their past and in the possibility of its transformation into a living future.

HADITH AND SUNNAH

Many reform proposals have been advanced during the last decades, and many spiritual doctors have tried to devise a patent medicine for the sick body of Islam. But, until now, all was in vain, be cause all those clever doctors—at least those who get a hearing today—invariably forgot to prescribe, along with their medicines, tonics and elixirs, the natural *diet* on which the early development of the patient had been based. This diet, the only one which the body of Islam, sound or sick, can positively accept and assimilate, is the *Sunnah* of our Prophet Muhammad (peace and blessings be upon him). The *Sunnah* is the key to the under standing of the Islamic rise more than thirteen centuries ago ; and why should it not be a key to the understanding of our present degeneration? Observance of the *Sunnah* is synonymous with Islamic existence and progress. Neglect of the *Sunnah* is synonymous with decomposition and decay of Islam. The *Sunnah* was the iron framework of the House of Islam ; and if you remove the framework a building can you be surprised if it breaks down like a house of cards?

This simple truth, almost unanimously accepted by all leaned men throughout Islamic history, is—we know it well—most unpopular today for reasons connected with the ever-growing influence of Western civilization. But it is truth nonetheless, and in fact, the only truth which can save us from the chaos and the shame of our present decay.

The word *Sunnah* is used here in its widest meaning, namely, the example the Prophet has set before us in his actions and sayings. His wonderful life was a living illustration and explanation of the Qur'ãn, and we can do no greater justice to the Holy Book than by following him who was the means of its revelation.

We have seen that one of the main achievements of Islam, the one which distinguishes it from all other transcendental systems, is the complete reconciliation between the moral and the material sides of human life. This was one of the reasons why Islam in its prime had such a triumphant success wherever it appeared. It brought to mankind the new message that the earth need not be despised in order that heaven be gained. This prominent feature of Islam explains why our Prophet, in his mission as an apostolic guide of humanity, was so deeply concerned with human life in its polarity both as a spiritual and a material phenomenon. It does not, therefore, show a very deep understanding of Islam if some one discriminates between such orders of the Prophet as deal with purely devotional and spiritual matters, and others which have to do with questions of our society and our daily life. The contention that we are obliged to follow the commands belonging to the first group, but not obliged to follow those of the second, is as superficial and, in its spirit, as anti-Islamic as the idea that certain general injunctions of the Qur'ãn were meant only for the ignorant Arabs at the time of the revelation, and not for the refined gentlemen of the twentieth century. At its root lies a strange under-estimation of the prophetical role of Mustafa.

As the life of a Muslim must be directed upon a full and unreserved co-operation between his spiritual and his bodily Self, so the leadership of our Prophet embraces life as a compound entity, a sum total of moral and practical, individual and social manifestations. This is the deepest meaning of *Sunnah.* The Qur'ãn says:

وَمَآ اٰتٰكُمُ الرَّسُوْلُ فَخُذُوْهُ ۚ وَمَانَهٰكُمْ عَنْهُ فَانْتَهُوْا ۚ
(الحشر: ٧)

"Whatever the Prophet enjoins you, accept; and whatever he forbids you, avoid" (*Hashar* : 7). And the Prophet said

تفرقت اليهود على احد وسبعين فرقة وتفرقت النصارى على اثنين وسبعين فرقة وستفرق امتى على ثلاث وسبعين فرقة
(سنن ابى داؤد ترمذى)

"The Jews have been split up into seventy-one sects, the Christians into seventy-two sects, and the Muslims will be split up into seventy-three sects" *(Sunan Abi Da'ud, Jami ''at-Tirmidhi, Sunan ad-Darimi, Musnad Ibn Hanbal)*. In this connection it may be mentioned that in Arabian usage the number 70 very often stands for "many", and does not necessarily denote the actual arithmetical figure. So the Prophet obviously intended to say that the sects and divisions among the Muslims would be very many, even more than those among the Jews and Christians. And he added :

كلهم فى النار الا واحدة

"all of them are destined for the Fire with the exception of one." When the Companions asked which one would be the one, the right-guided group, he answered :

ما انا عليه و اصحابى

"That which is based on my and my Companion's Sunnah". Certain verses of the Qur'ãn make this point clear beyond any possibility of misunderstanding

فَلَا وَرَبِّكَ لَا يُؤْمِنُوْنَ حَتّٰى يُحَكِّمُوْكَ فِيْمَا شَجَرَ بَيْنَهُمْ ثُمَّ لَا يَجِدُوْا فِيْٓ

اَنْفُسِهِمْ حَرَجًا مِّمَّا قَضَيْتَ وَيُسَلِّمُوْا تَسْلِيْمًا (النساء : ٦٥)

"Nay, by thy Sustainer! they do not attain to faith until they make thee (O Muhammad) a judge of what is in dispute between them and find in themselves no dislike of what thou decidest, and submit with (full) submission" *(Nisa :* 65). And:

قُلْ اِنْ كُنْتُمْ تُحِبُّوْنَ اللّٰهَ فَاتَّبِعُوْنِيْ يُحْبِبْكُمُ اللّٰهُ وَيَغْفِرْ لَكُمْ ذُنُوْبَكُمْ ط

وَاللّٰهُ غَفُوْرٌ رَّحِيْمٌ (٣١) قُلْ اَطِيْعُوا اللّٰهَ وَالرَّسُوْلَ ۚ فَاِنْ تَوَلَّوْا فَاِنَّ

اللّٰهَ لَا يُحِبُّ الْكٰفِرِيْنَ (آل عمرٰن : ٣١-٣٢)

"Say (O Muhammad) : If you love God, follow me: God will love you and forgive you your sins ; and God is Forgiving, a Dispenser of Grace. Say : Obey God and the Apostle ! But if they turn away, behold, God loveth not the Unbelievers"

(Al-Imran :31, 32).

The Sunnah of the Prophet is, therefore, next to the Qur'ān, the second source of Islamic law of social and personal behaviour. In fact, we must regard the *Sunnah* as *the only valid explanation* of the Qur'ãnic teachings, the only means to avoid dissensions concerning their interpretation and adaptation to practical use. Many verses of the Holy Qur'ãn have an allegorical meaning and could be understood in different ways unless there was some definite system of interpretation. And there are, furthermore, many items of practical importance not explicitly dealt with in the Qur'ãn. The spirit prevailing in the Holy Book is, to be sure, uniform throughout ; but to deduce from it the practical attitude which we have to adopt is not in every case an easy matter. So long as we believe that this Book is the Word of God, perfect in form and purpose, the only logical conclusion is that it never was intended to be used independently of the personal guidance of the Prophet which is embodied in the system of *Sunnah*. In the next chapter an attempt will be made to explain the ultimate reasons for the linking up of the Qur'ãn, for all times, with the inspiring and directing personality of the Prophet.

For the purposes of this chapter the following reflection should be sufficient. Our reasoning tells us that there could not possibly be a better interpreter of the Qur'ãnic teachings than he through whom they were revealed to humanity.

The slogan we so often hear in our days, "Let us go back to the Qur'ãn, but let us not be slavish followers of the *Sunnah*," merely betrays an ignorance of Islam. Those who speak so, resemble a man who wishes to enter a palace but does not wish to employ the genuine key which alone is fit to open the door.

And so we come to the very important question as to the authenticity of the sources which reveal the life and the sayings of the Prophet to us. These sources are the *Ahadith,* the Traditions of the sayings and actions of the Prophet reported and transmitted by his Companions and critically collected in the first few centuries of Islam. Many modern Muslims profess that they would be ready to follow the *Sunnah* ; but they think they cannot rely upon the body of the *Ahadith* on which it rests.

It has become a matter of fashion in our days to deny, in principle, the authenticity of *Ahadith* and therefore, of the whole structure of the *Sunnah*.

Is there any scientific warrant for this attitude? Is there any scientific justification for the rejection of *Ahadith* as a dependable source of Islamic Law?

We should think that the opponents of orthodox thought would be able to bring forward really convincing arguments which would establish, once for all, the unreliability of the Traditions ascribed to the Prophet. But this is not the case. In spite of all the efforts which have been employed to challenge the authenticity of *Hadith* as a body, those modern critics, both Eastern and Western, have not been able to back their purely temperamental criticism with results of scientific research. It would be rather difficult to do so, as the compilers of the early *hadith*-collections, and particularly the Imams Bukhari and Muslim have done whatever was humanly possible to put the authenticity of every Tradition to a very rigorous test—a far more rigorous test than European historians usually apply to any historical document.

It would go far beyond the limit of this book to dwell here in detail on the scrupulous method by which the reliability of Traditions was investigated by the early *Muhaddithun*, the learned men devoted to the study of *Hadith*. For our purpose it may suffice to say that a complete science has been evolved, the only object of which is the research as to the meaning, the form and the way of transmission of the Prophet's *Ahadith*. An historical branch of this science succeeded in establishing an unbroken chain of detailed biographies of all those personalities who have ever been mentioned as narrators of Traditions. The lives of those men and women have been thoroughly investigated from every point of view, and only those have been accepted as reliable whose way of life and of transmitting a *Hadith* perfectly responds to the standard stipulated by the great *Muhaddithum* and believed to be the most exacting that could be conceived. If, therefore, anyone wishes to contest today the authenticity of a particular *Hadith* or of the system as a whole, the burden of proving its inaccuracy falls upon him alone. It is scientifically not in the least justifiable to contest the veracity of an historical source unless one is prepared to prove that this source is defective. If not reasonable, that is, scientific, argument can be found against the veracity of the source itself or against one or more of its later transmitters, and if, on the other hand, no other contradictory report about the same matter exists, then we are bound to accept the Traditions as true.

Suppose, for example, when some one speaks about the Indian wars of Mahmud of Ghazna, you suddenly get up and say : "I don't believe that Mahmud ever came to India. It is a legend without historical foundation". What would happen in such a case ? At once some person well-versed in history would try to correct your mistake and would quote chronicles and histories, based on reports of contemporaries of that famous Sultan, as a definite proof of the fact that Mahmud *had* been in India. In that case you would have to accept the proof—or you would be regarded as a crank who for no obvious reason to deny solid historical facts. If this is so, one must ask oneself why our modern critics do not extend the same logical fairmindedness to the problem of *Ahadith* as well.

The primary ground for a *Hadith* being false would be a willful lie on the part of the first source, the Companions concerned, or of the later transmitters. As to the Companions, such a possibility can be ruled out *a priori*. It requires only some insight into the psychological side of the problem in order to relegate such assumptions into the sphere of pure fancy. The tremendous impression which the personality of the Prophet has made on these men and women is an outstanding fact of human history ; and moreover, it is extremely well *documented* by history. Is it conceivable that people who were ready to sacrifice themselves and all they possessed at the bidding of the Apostle of God would play tricks with his words ? The Prophet had said : من كذب على متعمدا فليتبوا مقعده من النار

(ابی داؤد، ترمذی، ابن ماجه صحیح البخاری)

"Whoever intentionally lies about me will take his place in the Fire" *(Sahih al-Bukhari, Sunan Abi Da'ud, Jami at-Tirmidhi, Sunan Ibn Majah, Sunan ad-Darimi, Musnad Ibn Hanbal).* This the Companions fully knew; they believed implicitly in the words of the Prophet whom they regarded as the Speaker of God ; and is it probable, from the psychological point of view, that they disregarded this very definite injunction ?

In criminal court proceedings the first "question facing the judge is *cui bono*—for "whose benefit—the crime could have been committed. This judicial principle can be applied to the problem of *Hadith* as well. With the exception of Traditions which directly concern the status of certain individuals or groups, for example, the decidedly spurious—and by most of the *Muhaddithun* rejected—Traditions connected with the political claims of the different parties in the first century after the Prophet's death, there could have been no "profitable" reason for any individual to falsify sayings of the Prophet. It was in a just appreciation of the possibility of *Ahadith* being invented for some personal ends that the two foremost authorities among the Traditionalists, the Imams Bukhari and Muslim have rigorously excluded all Traditions relating to party politics from their compilations. What remained was fairly beyond the suspicion of giving personal advantages to anyone.

There is one argument more on which the authenticity of a *Hadith* could be challenged. It is conceivable that either the Companion who heard it from the lips of the Prophet or one or another of the later narrators has committed—while being subjectively truthful—a mistake due to a misunderstanding of the Prophet's words, or a lapse of memory, or some other psychological reason. But the internal, that is, psychological, evidence speaks against any great possibility of such mistakes, at least on the part of the Companions. To the people who lived with the Prophet, each one of his sayings and actions was of utmost significance, due not only to the fascination which his personality exerted on them but also to their firm belief that it was God's will that they should regulate their life, even in its minute details, according to the direction and the example of the Prophet. Therefore they could not take the question of his sayings offhand, but tried to preserve them in their memory even at the cost of great personal discomforts. It is related that the Companions who were immediately associated with the Prophet made among themselves .groups of two men each one of whom was to be alternately in the vicinity of the Prophet while the other was busy with the pursuit of his livelihood or other matters ; and whatever they heard or saw of their Master they communicated to each other : so anxious were they lest some saying or doing of the Prophet should escape their notice. It is not very probable that, with such an attitude, they could have been negligent as to the exact wording of a *Hadith.* And if it was possible for hundreds of Companions to preserve the wording of the whole Qur'ãn, down to the smallest details of spelling, in their memory, then it was, no doubt, equally possible for them and for those who immediately followed them to keep single sayings of the Prophet in their memory without adding to them or omitting anything from them.

Moreover, the Traditionists ascribe perfect authenticity to those *Ahadith* only which are reported in the same form through different, independent chains of narrators. Nor is this all. In order to be *Sahih* (sound), a *Hadith* must be corroborated at every stage of transmission by the independent evidence of at least two, and possibly more, transmitters—so that at no stage the report should hinge on the authority of one person only demand of corroboration is so exacting that in a *Hadith* reported through, say, three "generations" of transmitters between the Companions concerned and the final compiler, actually a score or more of transmitters, distributed over those three "generations", are involved.

With all this, no Muslim has ever believed that Traditions of the Prophet could have the status, or even the undisputed authenticity, of the Qur'ãn. At no time the critical investigation of *Hadith* has stopped. The fact that there are numberless spurious *Ahadith* did not in the least escape the attention of the *Muhaddithun,* as European critics naively seem to suppose. On the contrary, the critical science of *Hadith* was initiated by the necessity of discerning between authentic and spurious, and the very Imams Bukhari and Muslim, not to mention the lesser Traditionists, are direct products of this critical attitude. The existence, therefore, of false *Ahadith* does not prove anything against the system of *Hadith* as a whole—no more than a fanciful tale from the *Arabian Nights* could be regarded as an argument against the authenticity of any historical report of the corresponding period.

Until now no critic has been able to prove in a systematic way that the body of *Hadith* regarded as authentic according to the test-standard of the foremost Traditions is inaccurate. The rejection of authentic Traditions, either as a whole or in parts, is so far a purely temperamental matter, and has failed to establish itself as the result of unprejudiced, scientific investigation. But the motive for such an oppositional attitude among many Muslims of our time can easily be traced. This motive lies in the impossibility of bringing our present, degenerate ways of living and thinking into line with the true spirit of Islam as reflected in the *Sunnah* of our Prophet. In order to justify their own shortcomings and the shortcomings of their environment, those pseudo-critics of *Hadith* try to remove the necessity of following the *Sunnah;* because, if this were done, they would be able to interpret the Qur'ãnic teachings just as they like, on the lines of superficial "rationalism"—that is, every one according to his own inclination and turn of mind. And in this way the exceptional position of Islam as a moral and practical, as an individual and social code, would be shattered to pieces.

In these days, when the influence of Western civilization makes itself more and more felt in Muslim countries, one motive more is added to the strange attitude of the so-called "Muslim intelligentsia" in this matter. It is impossible to live according to the *Sunnah* of our Prophet and to follow the Western mode of life at one and the same time. But the present generation of Muslims is ready to adore everything that is Western, to worship the foreign civilization because it is foreign, powerful and materially brilliant. This "Westernisation" is the stronger reason why the Traditions of our Prophet and, along with them, the whole structure of the *Sunnah* have become so unpopular today. The *Sunnah* is so obviously opposed to the fundamental ideas underlying Western civilization that those who are fascinated by the latter see no way out of the tangle but to describe the *Sunnah* as an irrelevant, and therefore not compulsory, aspect of Islam—because it is "based on unreliable Traditions". After that, it becomes easier to twist the teachings of the Qur'ãn in such a way that they appear to suit the spirit of Western civilization.

THE SPIRIT OF THE SUNNAH

Almost as important as the formal, so to say legal, justification of the *Sunnah* through the establishment of the historical dependability of *Hadith* is the question as to its inner, spiritual justification. Why should an observance of the *Sunnah* be regarded as indispensable for a life in the true sense of Islam ? Is there no other way to the reality of Islam than through that large system of actions and customs, of orders and prohibitions, some of them of an obviously trivial nature, but all of them derived from the life-example of the Prophet? No doubt, he was the greatest of men ; but is not the necessity to imitate his life in all its formal details an infringement on the individual freedom of human personality ? It is an old objection which unfriendly critics of Islam usually put forward that the necessity of strictly following the *Sunnah* was one of the main causes of the subsequent decay of the Islamic world, for such an attitude is supposed to encroach, in the long run, on the liberty of human action and the natural development of society. It is of the greatest importance for the future of Islam whether we are able to meet this objection or not. Our attitude towards the problem of the *Sunnah* will determine our future attitude towards Islam.

We are proud, and justly proud, of the fact that Islam, as a religion, is not based on mystic dogmatism but is always open to the critical inquiry of reason. We have, therefore, the right not only to know that the observance of the *Sunnah* has been imposed upon us but also to understand the inherent reason of its imposition.

Islam leads man to a unification of all aspects of life. Being a means to that goal, this religion represents in itself a totality of conceptions to which nothing can be added and from which nothing can be subtracted. There is no room for electicism in Islam. Wherever its teachings are recognised as really pronounced by the Qur'ãn or the Prophet we must accept them in their completeness ; otherwise they lose their value. It is a fundamental misunderstanding of Islam to think that being a religion of reason, it leaves its teachings open to individual selection—a claim made possible by a popular misconception of "rationalism". There is a wide—and by the philosophy of all ages sufficiently recognised gulf between reason and "rationalism" as it is commonly understood today. The function of reason in regard to religious teaching is of a controlling character ; its duty is to watch that nothing is imposed on the human mind which it cannot bear easily, that is, without the aid of philosophical juggleries. So far as Islam is concerned, unprejudiced reason has, time and again, given it its unreserved vote of confidence. That does not mean that every one who gets in touch with Islam will necessarily accept its teachings as obliging for himself ; this is a matter of temperament and—last, but not least—of spiritual illumination. But surely and certainly no unbiased person would contend that there is anything in Islam contrary to reason. No doubt, there are things in it beyond the limits of human understanding ; but nothing which is contrary to it.

The role of reason in religious matters is, as we have seen, in the nature of a control —a registration apparatus saying "yes" or "no", as the case may be. But this is not the case with so-called "rationalism". It does not content itself with registration and control, but jumps into the field of speculation ; it is not receptive and detached like pure reason, but extremely subjective and temperamental. Reason knows its own limits ; but "rationalism" is preposterous in its claim to encompass the world and all mysteries within its own individual circle. In religious matters it hardly even concedes the possibility of certain things being, temporarily or permanently, beyond human understanding ; but it is, at the same time, illogical enough to concede this possibility to science— and so to itself.

Over-estimation of this unimaginative rationalism is one of the causes why so many modern Muslims refuse to surrender themselves to the guidance of the Prophet. But it does not need a Kant today to prove that human understanding is strictly limited in its possibilities. Our mind is unable, by virtue of its nature, to understand the idea of *totality* we can grasp, of all things, their details only. We do not know what infinity or eternity is ; we do not even know what life is. In problems of a religion resting on transcendental foundations we, therefore, need a guide whose mind possesses something more than the normal reasoning qualities and the subjective rationalism common to all of us ; we need someone who is inspired—in one word, a Prophet. If we believe that the Qur'ãn is the Word of God, and that Muhammad (peace and blessings upon him) was God's Apostle, we are not only morally but also intellectually bound to follow his guidance blindly. The expression "blindly" does not mean that we should exclude our powers of reasoning. On the contrary, we have to make use of those powers to the best of our ability and knowledge ; we have to try to discover the inherent meaning and purpose of the commands transmitted to us by the Prophet. But in any case—whether we are able to understand its ultimate purpose or not—we must obey the order. I should like to illustrate this by the example of a soldier who has been ordered by his general to occupy a certain strategic position. The good soldier will follow and execute the order immediately. If, while doing so, he is able to explain to himself the ultimate strategic purpose which the general had in view, the better for him and for his career ; but if the deeper aim which underlies the general's command does not reveal itself to him at once, he is nevertheless not entitled to give up or even to postpone its execution. We Muslims rely upon our Prophet's being the best commander mankind could ever get. We naturally believe that he knew the domain of religion both in its spiritual and its social aspect far better than we ever could. In ordering us to do this or to avoid that, he always had some "strategic" objective in view which he thought to be indispensable for the spiritual or social welfare of man. Sometimes this object is clearly visible, and sometimes it is more or less hidden before the untrained eyes of the average man ; sometimes we can understand the deepest aim of the Prophet's order, and sometimes only the superficial, immediate purpose. Whatever the case may be, we are bound to follow' the Prophet's commands, provided their authenticity is reasonably established. Nothing else matters. Of course, there are commands of the Prophet which are obviously of paramount importance and others which are less important, and we have to give the more important precedence over the less important. But never have we the right to disregard any one of them because they appear to us "unessential"—for it is said in the Qur'ãn of the Prophet :

وما ينطق عن الهوى (النجم : ٣)

"He does not speak of his own desire"

(*Najam:* 53:3).

That is, he speaks only when an objective *necessity* arises ; and he does it because God orders him to do so. And for this reason we are obliged to follow the Prophet's *Sunnah* in spirit *and* in form, if we wish to be true to the spirit of Islam.

Once the objective necessity, for a Muslim, to follow the *Sunnah* of the Prophet is established, he has the right, even the duty, to inquire into its role within the religious and social structure of Islam. What is the spiritual meaning of that great, detailed system of laws and rules of conduct which are supposed to pervade the life of a Muslim from his birth to the moment of death, and to regulate his behaviour in the most important as well as in the most insignificant phases of his existence ? Or is there, perhaps, no meaning at all ? Was there any good in the Prophet's ordering his followers to do everything in the way he did it ? What difference can it make whether I eat with the right or with the left hand—if both are equally clean ? What 'difference, whether I grew my beard or shave it ? Are such things not purely formal ? Have they any bearing on the progress of man or on the welfare of society ? And if not, why have they been imposed on us ?

It is high time for us, who believe that Islam stands and falls with the observance of the *Sunnah,* to answer the questions.

There are, to my knowledge, at least three distinct reasons for the institution of *Sunnah.*

The first reason is the training of man, in a methodical way, to live permanently in a state of consciousness, wakefulness and self-control. In the spiritual progress of man, haphazard actions and habits are like stumbling blocks in the way of a racing horse ; they must be reduced to a minimum, because they destroy spiritual concentration. Everything we do should be determined by our will and submitted to our moral control. But in order to be able to do so we must learn to *observe* ourselves. This necessity, for a Muslim of permanent self-control has been beautifully expressed by 'Umar ibn al-Khattab :

حاسبوا انفسكم قبل أن تحاسبوا

"Render to yourself account about yourselves before you are called upon to render account." And the Prophet said

اعبد ربك كأنك تراه

(صحيح البخاری، مسلم)

"Worship thy Lord as if thou saw Him" *(Sahih al- Bukhari, Sahih Muslim, Sunan Abi Da'ud, Sunan an-Nasã'i).*

It has been pointed out before that the Islamic idea of worship embraces not only the strictly devotional duties but actually the whole of our life. Its goal is the unification of our spiritual and our material Selves into one single entity. Our endeavours must be, therefore, clearly directed towards the elimination of the unconscious, uncontrolled factors in our life as much as this is humanly possible. Self-observation is the first step on this way ; and the sure method to train oneself in self-observation is to get the habitual, seemingly unimportant, actions of our daily life under control. Those "small" things, those "unimportant" actions and habits are in the context of the mental training we are speaking of, in reality far more important than the "great" activities in our life. The great things are always, by virtue of their greatness, clearly visible and therefore they mostly remain within the sphere of consciousness. But those other, those "small" things easily escape our attention and cheat our control. Therefore they are by far the more valuable objects on which we can sharpen our powers of self-control.

It might be perhaps, in itself, not important with which hand we eat or whether we shave or grew our beard : but it is psychologically of the highest importance to do things according to a systematic resolve: for by doing so we grew ourselves keyed up to a high pitch of self-observation and moral control. This is not an easy matter —for, laziness of the mind is no less real than laziness of the body. If you ask a man who is accustomed to a sedentary mode of life to walk a long distance, he will soon grow tired and be unable to proceed further. But not so a man who throughout the whole of his life has trained himself in walking. For him this kind of muscular exertion is no exertion at all ; it is a pleasant bodily action to which he is accustomed.

This is a further explanation why the *Sunnah* covers almost every aspect of human life. If we are constantly called upon to subject all our actions and omissions to conscious discrimination, our power of self-observation grows readily and in time becomes our second nature. Every day, as long as this training proceeds, our moral laziness diminishes along with it.

The use of the expression "training" naturally implies that its result is dependent on the *consciousness* of its performance. The moment the practice of the *Sunnah* degenerates into mechanical routine it entirely loses its educative value. Such has been the case with the Muslims during the last centuries. When the Companions of the Prophet and the generations which succeeded them made the attempt to conform every detail of their existence to the example of the Master, they did it in conscious surrender to a directive will, that would shape their life in the' spirit of the Qur'ãn. Owing to this conscious resolve they could benefit by the training through *Sunnah* to the full extent. It is not the fault of the system if the Muslims of later times did not make the right use of the psychological avenues it opened. This omission was probably due, in a very large measure, to the influence of Sufism with its more or less pronounced contempt of the active and its emphasis on the purely receptive energies in man. As the practice of *Sunnah* had been already established as a component of Islamic religious life since the beginning of Islam, Sufism did not succeed in uprooting it in principle. But it succeeded in neutralising its active vigour and so, to a certain extent, its utility. The *Sunnah* remained, for the Sufis, an ideogram of only Platonic importance, with a mystical background; for the theologians and legists, a system of laws ; and for the Muslim masses nothing but a hollow shell without any living meaning. But notwithstanding the failure of the Muslims to benefit from the teachings of the Holy Qur'ãn and their interpretation through the *Sunnah* of the Prophet, the idea underlying the teachings as well as their interpretation has remained intact, and there is no reason why it could not be put into practice once again. The real objective of the *Sunnah* is not, as our antagonistic critics presume, the breeding of Pharisees and dry formalists, but of conscious, determined, deep-hearted men of action. Men and women of such a style were the Companions of the Prophet. The permanent consciousness, inner wakefulness and sense of responsibility in all they did—therein lies the secret of their miraculous efficiency and their startling historical success.

This is the first and, so to say, individual aspect of the *Sunnah*. Its second aspect is its social importance and utility. There can be hardly any doubt that most of the social conflicts are due to men's misunderstanding each other's actions and intentions. The cause of such a misunderstanding is the extreme variety of temperaments and inclinations in the individual members of the society. Now different temperaments force different habits on men, and those different habits, hardened through the usage of long years, become barriers between individuals. If, on the contrary, several individuals happen to have identical habits throughout their life, there is every probability of their mutual relations being sympathetic and their minds ready to understand each other. Therefore Islam, which is equally concerned with social as well as with individual welfare makes it an essential point that the individual members of the society should be systematically induced to make their habits and customs resemble each other, however different their social or economic status be in each case.

But beyond this, the *Sunnah* in its so-called "rigidity" renders even a greater service to society; it make it coherent and stable in form and precludes the development of antagonisms and conflicts such as have, under the name of "social questions", caused a considerable confusion in Western society. Such social questions arise when certain institutions or customs are felt to be imperfect or defective, and are therefore open to criticism and progressive changes. But for the Muslims—that is for those who consider themselves bound by the Law of the Qur'ãn and, consequently, by the injunctions given by the Prophet—the conditions of the society must have a settled appearance, because they are supposed to be of transcendental origin. As long as there is no doubt as to this origin, no need and no desire will arise to question the social organisation in its fundamentals. It is only thus that we can conceive a practical possibility for the Qur'ãnic postulate that the Muslims should be like a "solid building" (بنيان مرصوص). If we apply this principle to our communal life, there should be no necessity for the society to spend its energies on side-issues and partial "reforms" which, owing to their very nature, can have only passing value. Freed from dialectical confusion and built on the solid pedestal of the Divine Law and the life-example of our Prophet, Islamic society could use all its forces on problems of real material and intellectual welfare, thus paving the way for the individual in his spiritual endeavour. This, and nothing else, is the real religious objective of the

Islamic social organisation.

And now we come to the third aspect of the *Sunnah* and the necessity of our strictly following it.

In this system many details of our daily life are based on the example set by the Prophet. Whatever we do, we are permanently compelled to think of a corresponding doing or saying of the Prophet. Thus the personality of the Greatest Man becomes deeply embodied in the very routine of our daily life, and his spiritual influence is made a real, ever-recurring factor in our existence. Consciously and subconsciously we are led to study the Prophet's attitude in this or that matter. We learn to regard him not only as the bearer of a moral revelation but also as the guide towards a perfect life. It is here that we must decide whether we wish to regard the Prophet as a mere wise man among many other wise men, or as the supreme Messenger of God' always acting under Divine inspiration. The view-point of the Holy Qur'ãn in this matter is clear beyond any possibility of misunderstanding. A man who is designed as the Last of the Prophets and a "Mercy to the Worlds" cannot be but permanently inspired. To reject his guidance, or certain elements of it, would mean nothing less than to reject or under-estimate God's own guidance. It would mean further, in the logical continuation of this thought, that the entire message of Islam was not intended to be a final, but only an *alternative* solution of man's problems, and that it is left to our discretion to choose this or some other, perhaps equally true and useful, solution. This easy—because morally and practically not in the least obliging—principle might lead us anywhere, but surely not to the spirit of Islam, of which it is said in the Qur'ãn

اَلْيَوْمَ اَكْمَلْتُ لَكُمْ دِيْنَكُمْ وَاَتْمَمْتُ عَلَيْكُمْ نِعْمَتِيْ وَرَضِيْتُ لَكُمُ الْاِسْلَامَ دِيْنًا ط . (المائده:٣)

"Today I have made perfect for you your religion, and fulfilled My favour unto you, and chosen Islam as your religion" *(Maiedah* : 3).

We regard Islam as superior to all other religious systems because it embraces life in its totality. It takes World and Hereafter, soul and body, individual and society, equally into consideration. It takes into consideration not only the lofty possibilities of the human nature but also its inherent limitations and weaknesses. It does not impose the impossible upon us, but directs us how to make the best use of our possibilities and so reach a higher plane of reality where there is no cleavage and no antagonism between Idea and Action. It is not a way among others, but *the* way ; and the Man who gave us this teaching is not just one guide among others, but *the* guide. To follow all he did and ordered is to follow Islam; to discard his *Sunnah* is to discard the reality of Islam.

CONCLUSION

In the foregoing I have tried to show that Islam, in its true meaning, cannot benefit by an assimilation of Western civilization. But, on the other hand, the Muslim world has today so little energy left that it does not offer sufficient resistance. The remnants of its cultural existence are being everywhere levelled to the ground under the pressure of Western ideas and customs. A note of resignation is audible ; and resignation, in the life of nations and cultures means death.

What is the matter with Islam ? Is it really, as our adversaries and the defeatists within our own ranks will make us believe a "spent force" ? Has it outlived its own usefulness and given to the world all it had to give ?

History tells us that all human cultures and civilizations are organic entities and resemble living beings. They run through all the phases organic life is bound to pass : they are born, they have youth, ripe age, and at the end comes decay. Like plants that wither and fall to dust, cultures die at the end of their time and give room to others, freshly born ones.

Is this the case with Islam ? It would appear so at the first superficial look. No doubt, Islamic culture has had its splendid rise and its blossoming age, it had power to inspire men to deeds and sacrifices, it transformed nations and changed the face of the earth ; and later it stood still and became stagnant, and then it became an empty word, and at present we witness its utter debasement and decay. But is this all?

If we believe that Islam is not a mere culture among many others, not a mere outcome of human thoughts and endeavours, but a Law decreed by God Almighty to be followed by humanity at all times and everywhere, then the aspect changes thoroughly. If Islamic culture is or was the result of our following a revealed Law, we can never admit that, like other cultures, it is chained to the lapse of time and limited to a particular period. What appears to be the decay of Islam is in reality nothing but the death and the emptiness of our hearts which are too idle and too lazy to hear the eternal voice. No sign is visible that mankind, in its present stature, has outgrown Islam. It has not been able to produce a better system of ethics than that expressed in Islam; it has not been able to put the idea of human brotherhood on a practical footing, as Islam did in its supra-national concept of '*ummah*', it has not been able to create a social structure in which the conflicts and frictions between its members are as efficiently reduced to a minimum as in the social plan of Islam ; it has not been able to enhance the dignity of man ; his feeling of security ; his spiritual hope ; and last, but surely not least, his happiness.

In all these things the present achievements of the human race fall considerably short of the Islamic programme. Where, then, is the justification for saying that Islam is "out of date" ? Is it only because its foundations are purely religious, and religious orientation is out of fashion today ? But if we see that a system based on religion has been able to evolve a practical programme of life more complete, more concrete and more congenial to man's psychological constitution than any other thing the human mind has been able to produce by way of reforms and proposals—is not just this a very weighty argument in favour of a religious outlook ?

Islam, we have every reason to believe, has been fully vindicated by the positive achievements of man, because it has envisaged them and pointed them out as desirable long before they were attained ; and equally well it has been vindicated by the shortcomings, errors and pitfalls of human development, because it has loudly and clearly warned against them long before mankind recognised them as errors. Quite apart from one's religious beliefs, there is, from a purely intellectual view-point, every inducement to follow confidently the practical guidance of Islam.

If we consider our culture and civilization from this point of view we necessarily come to the conclusion that its revival is possible. We need not "reform" Islam, as some Muslims think—for it is already perfect in itself. What we must reform is our attitude towards religion, our laziness, our one word, *our* defects, and not some supposed defects of Islam. In order to attain to an Islamic revival we need not search for new principles of conduct from outside, but have only to apply the old and forsaken ones. We certainly may receive new impulses from foreign cultures, but we cannot substitute the perfect fabric of Islam by anything non-Islamic, may it come from the West or from the East. Islam, as a spiritual and social institution, cannot be "improved". In these circumstances, any change in its conceptions or its social organisation caused by the intrusion of foreign cultural influences is in reality retrograde and destructive, and therefore to be deeply regretted. A change there must be : but it should be a change from *within ourselves*—and it should go in the direction of Islam, and not away from it.

But with all this, we must not deceive ourselves. We know that our world, the world of Islam, has almost lost its reality as an independent cultural factor. I am not speaking here of the political aspect of Muslim decay. By far the most important feature of our present-day condition is to be found in the intellectual and social spheres : in the disappearance of our belief and the disruption of our social organism. Very little seems to have remained of the original soundness which, as we have seen, was such a peculiar characteristic of early Islamic society. The state of cultural and social chaos through which we are passing at present distinctly shows that the balancing forces which once were responsible for the greatness of the Islamic world are nearly exhausted today. We are drifting ; and no one knows to what cultural end. No intellectual courage remains, no will to resist or to avert that torrent of foreign influences destructive to our religion and society. We have thrown aside the best moral teachings the world has ever seen. We belie our faith, whereas to our forefathers it was a living urge ; we are ashamed, whereas they were proud ; we are mean and self-centered, whereas they generously opened themselves out to the world ; we are empty, whereas they were full.

This lamentation is well-known to every thinking Muslim. Every one has heard it repeated many times. Is it any use then, one could ask, to have it repeated once more ? I think, it is. For there can be no outlet for us out of the shame of our decadence but one : to admit the shame, to have it day and night before our eyes and to taste its bitterness : until we resolve to remove its causes. It is no use to hide the grim truth from ourselves and to pretend that the world of Islam is growing in Islamic activity, that missions are working in four continents, that Western people realise more and more the beauty of Islam...... It is no use to pretend all this and to employ casuistic arguments in order to convince ourselves that our humiliation is not bottomless. For it *is* bottomless.

But shall this be the end ? It cannot be. Our longing for regeneration, the desire of so many of us to become better than we are at present, gives us the right to hope that it is not yet over with us. There *is* a way to regeneration, and this way is clearly visible to everyone who has eyes to see.

Our first step must be a shedding of that spirit of "apology" for Islam, which is only another name for intellectual defeatism : only a masquerade of our own scepticism. And the next stage must be our conscious, deliberate following of the *Sunnah* of our Prophet. For *Sunnah* means no more and no less than the teachings of Islam translated into practice. By applying it as an ultimate test to the requirements of our daily life we will easily recognise which impulses from Western civilization might be accepted and which are to be rejected. Instead of meekly submitting Islam to foreign intellectual norms, we must learn—once more—to regard *Islam* as the norm by which the world is to be judged.

It is true, however, that many of the original intentions of Islam have been brought into a false perspective through inadequate but nevertheless commonly accepted interpretation, and those of the Muslims who are not in a position to go back for themselves to the original sources and thus to readjust their conceptions are confronted with a partially distorted picture of Islam and things Islamic. The impracticable propositions which are today put forward by a self-styled "orthodoxy", as postulates of Islam are in most cases nothing but contentional interpretations of the original postulates on the basis of the old Neo-Platonic logic which might have been "modern", that is, workable in the second or third century of the Hijrah, but is extremely out-of-date now. The Muslim educated on Western lines, mostly unacquainted with Arabic and not well-versed in the intricacies *of fiqah,* is naturally prone to regard those worn-out, subjective interpretations and conceptions as reproducing the true intentions of the Law-Giver : and in his disappointment over their inadequacy he often draws back from what he supposes to be the canonical law *(shari'ah)* of Islam. Thus, in order that it may once again become a creative force in the life of Muslims, the valuation of the Islamic proposition must be revised in the light of our *own* understanding of the original sources and freed from the thick layer of conventional interpretations which have accumulated for centuries and have been found wanting in the present time. The outcome of such an endeavour might be the emergence of a new *fiqah,* exactly conforming to the Two Sources of Islam—the Qur'ān and the life-example of the Prophet— and at the same time answering to the exigencies of present life : just as the older forms *of fiqah* answered to the exigencies of a period dominated by Aristotelian and Neo-Platonic philosophy and to the conditions of life prevailing in those earlier ages.

But only if we regain our lost self-confidence can we expect to turn our way upwards once again. Never will the goal be reached if we destroy our own social institutions and imitate a foreign civilization— foreign not only in an historical or a geographical but also in a spiritual sense.

As things stand today, Islam is like a sinking ship. All hands that could help are needed on board. But it will be saved if the Muslims hear and understand the call of the Holy Qur'ān :

لقد كان لكم فى رسول الله اسوة حسنة لمن كان
يرجو الله واليوم الاخر (الاحزاب: ٢١)

"Verily in the Apostle of God you have the best example for everyone who looks forward towards God and the Day of Judgment" (*Ahzaab* 21).

COMMENTS

"This work is extremely interesting. I have no doubt that coming as it does from a highly cultured European convert to Islam it will prove an eye-opener to our younger generation."

Dr. Sir Muhammad Iqbal

"Mr. Muhammad Asad has written a book which is a notable contribution to what we may call the literature of Muslim regeneration, and the fact that he is a European by birth and education, a widely travelled and observant man, makes his achievement the more remarkable........It is the most thoughtful and thought-stimulating work on the means of Islamic revival that has appeared since Prince Sa'id Haleem Pasha's famous 'Islamlashmaq' ".

Marmaduke Pickthall,
in Islamic Culture (Hyderabad).

"A short but full book...... showing the errors of the Muslims with extraordinary clearness and wealth of argument."

Syed Sulaiman Nadvi, in Maarif (Azamgarh).

"A most interesting book........ Harsh words.... probably dictated more by determination to arouse than by a desire to scold. They represent a call to action to the youth of Islam which should attract the attention of our leaders."

Star of India (Calcutta).

"....a splendid production. I confess I never expected such a deep insight into the spirit of Islam from a new convert. The book ought to be most widely circulated. It must be in the hands of every educated Muslim youth."

Maulana Abdul Majid Daryabadi

"Muhammad Asad's book "ISLAM AT THE CROSS ROADS," I must say that it is a master-piece on the subject."

Maryam Jamila (Margrete Marx).

"..........May be classed among the best contributions recently made to the reconstructions of Muslim religious thought."

The Pioneer

THE AUTHOR

The Author Leopold Weiss (Muhammed Asad) was born in the Polish city of Lvov in 1900. He is the grand-son of an Orthodox Rabbi, and son of a lawyer. At the age of 13 he mastered Hebrew and Aramaic. His father desired him to become a rabbi, but he avoided this plan (without grieving his father). By his early twenties he could write and read the German, French, and Polish languages. He took to journalism and achieved quickly wide notice as an outstanding near Eastern correspondent to leading newspapers of the Continent, more especially as correspondent *of Frankfurter Zeitung* of Germany.

On visits to Arab and North African countries his interest grew to study the Muslim religion, Traditions and the Arabic language. He also travelled in Iran, Afghanistan, and other countries, and learned Persian. From there he proceeded to Berlin through Moscow and Poland, in 1926. Here he became a Muslim and named himself Muhammad Asad.

After his conversion he again travelled and worked throughout the Muslim world and stayed in Saudi Arabia for more than five years. During his sojourn he achieved prominence and enjoyed intimate friendship in the Arab countries, with great Arab leaders, such as the late king Ibn Saud of Saudi Arabia, the late King Raza Shah of Iran, the late King Abdullah of Jordan, and the Great Senusi of North Africa, and other prominent and

distinguished personages.
In 1932, he came to India and settled in Lahore (Pakistan). He wrote the book *Islam at the Cross-roads*. In Lahore he got the opportunity to meet the great Muslim thinker Dr. Sir Muhammad Iqbal, who was greatly impressed by his study of Islamic literature and asked Muhammad Asad to translate *Sahih al Bukhari* into English.
In 1939 he was interned by the British during the Second World War. On the termination of the war he was released. He then started to publish monthly *Arafat*.
After the partition of India he played an important part as an authority on Islamic Law, in setting up the New State of Pakistan. He also wrote a pamphlet entitled *Islamic Constitution Making*.
In 1953, he was appointed as Pakistan's Minister Plenipotentiary to the United Nations. After a year he left the post and published his impressions about Islam in *ROAD TO MAKKAH*, which was reproduced in some European and Asian languages.
In 1954, after completion of this book he left America and toured some states of the Continent and then went to Lebanon. In 1957 he was commissioned by the Government of Pakistan to organise an Islamic Colloquium. Next year he went to Switzerland and commenced translation of the Holy Qur'ãn into English, one-third of which came out in 1964 by the name of *MESSAGE OF THE QURAN*. Meanwhile he also wrote a book entitled *THE PRINCIPLES OF STATE AND GOVERNMENT IN ISLAM*.
In 1966 he was invited by the Saudi Government to Makkah to perform his seventh Hajj. He wrote his translation of the Qur'ãn.

www.ingramcontent.com/pod-product-compliance
Lightning Source LLC
Chambersburg PA
CBHW062138160726
48282CB00027B/866
* 9 7 8 9 3 9 4 7 7 0 1 5 7 *